POLITICAL CAMPAIGN PLAYBOOK

A practical guide to success in politics, government, elections, and life

David D. Roberts

Amazon KDP Inc. Publishing

Copyright © 2023 Amazon Inc. | KDP Publishing

All rights reserved

The characters and events portrayed in this book are fictitious. Any similarity to real persons, living or dead, is coincidental and not intended by the author.

No part of this book may be reproduced, or stored in a retrieval system, or transmitted in any form or by any means, electronic, mechanical, photocopying, recording, or otherwise, without express written permission of the publisher.

ISBN: 9798394726651

Library of Congress Control Number: 2018675309
Printed in the United States of America

To Those I Love - Mom, Dad, Lee, Amber, Staci, Tosha, Tyson, Jayce, Emma, Amber H., Cindy, Paiden, Brian, Haley, Cary, and Odie.

In memory of Ruby Fern Roberts.

CONTENTS

Title Page
Copyright
Dedication
PREFACE
POLITICAL CAMPAIGNS AND POLITICAL CAMPAIGN STRATEGIES — 1
YOUR POLITICAL PASSION — 5
CAMPAIGN PLANNING: YOUR OPENING PLAY — 7
YOUR POLITICAL CAMPAIGN PLAYBOOK: THE WINNING GAME PLAN — 10
BUILDING YOUR POLITICAL NETWORK AND MANAGING RELATIONSHIPS — 12
THE SPIRIT OF YOUR TEAM — 15
FORGING YOUR GAME PLAN WITH THE CANDIDATE — 18
PRE-GAME: PREPARATION AND PLANNING — 22
ANALYZING THE FIELD: UNDERSTANGING YOUR POLITICAL LANDSCAPE — 24
POLITICAL THEORY AND IDEOLOGY IN AMERICAN POLITICS — 26
DEFINING A WINNING STRATEGY — 32
WORKSHEET 2: DEFINING A WINNING STRATEGY — 34

OFFENSIVE PLAYS: DEVELOPING YOUR MESSAGE	35
ENGAGING WITH VOTERS	37
PLAYMAKING 101: TELLING YOUR STORY	40
YOUR GAMEPLAN – YOUR NARRATIVE	42
QUICKPLAY: MASTERING THE ONE-MINUTE STATEMENT	47
NAVIGATING THE INTRICACIES OF YOUR POLITICAL CAMPAIGN	52
THE ANATOMY OF THE HARD ASK	54
OFFENSIVE TACTIC: CRAFTING THE MESSAGE BOX	55
PLAYING DEFENSE: BALANCING CREDIBILITY AND CONTRAST	58
ANALYZING THE PLAYS: EFFECTIVE MESSAGING FROM OTHER CAMPAIGNS	60
PLAYING DIRTY: ATTACK ADS AND NEGATIVE CAMPAIGNING	62
GAME TIME: BRINGING IT ALL TOGETHER	68
FOCUSING ON THE RIGHT VOTERS	71
SCOUTING REPORT: YOUR CAMPAIGN'S TARGET AUDIENCE	75
WORKSHEETS: CREATING A COMPREHENSIVE TARGETING STRATEGY	77
INTEGRATING ALL TARGETING ELEMENTS: YOUR GAMEPLAN BLUEPRINT	79
CREATING AND LEADING A WINNING TEAM	81
CRAFTING A STRATEGIC VOTER ENGAGEMENT PLAN – YOUR FANBASE	86
PHONE BANKING	89
CANVASSING	92
DATA	96
BUILDING A STRONG FOUNDATION	98
NAVIGATING THE POLITICAL LANDSCAPE	101

COMMUNICATION AND THE ART OF PERSUASION	103
CAMPAIGN STRATEGY AND EXECUTION	106
COMMUNITY INVOLVEMENT AND GRASSROOTS ORGANIZING	108
EXPECTED CHALLENGES AND ADVERSITY IN POLITICS	115
THE IMPORTANCE OF ETHICS AND INTEGRITY	121
OVERCOMING BARRIERS AND CHALLENGES IN POLITICS	123
THE IMPORTANCE OF SELF-CARE	125
SCANDAL AND CRISIS MANAGEMENT AND ROLE OF THE MEDIA	127
About The Author	133
Praise For Author	135
Praise For Author	137
Books By This Author	139

PREFACE

It was on a scorching hot Fourth of July celebration in rural Southeastern Oklahoma that I discovered my passion for politics. Now, thirty years later, I've spent the entirety of that time continuing with some variation of what state senator Gene Stipe taught me along that parade route. We spent the day glad-handing our way down Main Street, me pulling a red Radio Flyer wagon complete with bumper stickers and pencils, him a top-of-his-game political leader that knew a child and a wagon make him appear humble and able to connect.

Today, I'd like to think I have more of a keen understanding of the intricacies of campaigns and the modern skill set to navigate the ever-changing political landscape. I've certainly been extremely fortunate, having been able to work alongside some of the most influential politicians and organizations of our time. Through these experiences, I have gained invaluable knowledge and insights that I now wish to share with young, aspiring public servants and political enthusiasts alike.

It had to have been those early experiences in campaigning and organizing that ultimately propelled me into politics and towards studying political science. It certainly ending up taking me on a journey where I walked many of the halls inside our world's corridors of power and rubbed elbows and provided my talents to numerous high-profile elected officials, candidates, and campaigns. Notable names include President Barack Obama, current-President Joe Biden, U.S. Senator Blanche Lincoln, Congressman Brad Carson, Governor Brad Henry, Governor Mike

Beebe, Congressman Mark Critz, and various stints with the DNC, DCCC, union-backed political action committees, and unions themselves. Currently, I am undertaking the task of developing this book while serving as the Director of Development and External Relations for the Oklahoma Democratic Party. I envision this book as something that will serve as a valuable resource for young high school and college students, first-time candidates and campaign managers as each of them take their first steps into the world of public service, running for office, or work in politics and government.

Reflecting on my journey, I can recall when, at one of my lower and more cynical states, and likely after several pitchers of beer, I cautioned a person interested in running for office plainly saying, "If I were your friend, I'd tell you that you shouldn't run. The money is awful, your wife or partner will hate you, and when you ultimately lose that initial race, as nearly every first time-candidate does, you'll be depressed, you'll have lost friends, and your future prospects outside of running again will be limited. Even just finding a job anywhere will probably be a challenge. All this without even beginning to discuss the intense scrutiny and hyper-intensified judgements that you'll face." He eventually laughed off my comment, but I must admit, there is actually a whole lot of truth to it.

Being in politics is demanding work. It lacks glamour and financial rewards, making it nearly impossible to balance a full-time job with a commute while raising a family. Almost every single process by which one becomes a public figure in government is intimidating. The usual filters that shield people from unkind remarks are gone to you forever the moment you step into the political arena. Politicians, plagued by a bruised-up reputation, attract frank criticism from their constituents and even their friends. This makes simple everyday encounters capable of turning into nightmares.

By becoming a candidate, every aspect of your life immediately shifts into, not simply being open for criticism, but a step further by almost welcoming scrutiny as folks who serve in many of the jobs I used to hold can't wait to crush you, sending you into the political abyss forever. You open it all up, not is safe - your family, business, past, relationships, demeanor, attitude, experience, dress, way of speaking, choice of words, platform, and ideas are all open to scrutiny. If you're an idealist at heart, sometimes you think an experience has caused you to loss a piece of your soul. And after one of the times you battle through all the process can throw and you and somehow you manage to win, the "fun" doesn't cease—it has then only began so prepare for it to start intensifying. *It's crucial to understand the challenges and realities, warts and all, before diving into the world of politics.*

Political Campaign Playbook is a comprehensive handbook designed to accommodate political novices and veterans, technical newbies and experts, career political operatives, and academics. The majority of the chapters can stand alone, allowing you to focus on specific aspects of a campaign or read the entire book cover to cover for a complete understanding. This guide is meant to be your roadmap, leading you to a successful political career, whether you aspire to run for office, work behind the scenes, or make a difference in your community through public service.

Throughout the chapters, you will find a perfect blend of strategic advice and practical tips to help you navigate the world of politics, government, and elections. We will explore topics such as negative campaigning, district and precinct analysis, digital and social media, traditional media, targeting voters, and managing campaign resources. Along the way, you'll learn the importance of understanding the legal aspects of campaigns, maintaining a positive tone, and staying true to your message.

As a candidate or campaign manager, it is crucial to know why you are running for office and to have a clear vision of what you hope to achieve. This book will help you define your objectives and develop a compelling message that resonates with your target audience. Furthermore, it will guide you in managing your expectations and navigating the challenges and triumphs of a political campaign.

Throughout your journey, remember to be vigilant of your campaign's tone and maintain a sophisticated approach to decision-making. The outcome of your campaign, whether successful or not, will leave a lasting impression on your community. By adhering to the principles outlined in this book, you will not only set yourself on the path to victory but also earn the respect and admiration of your constituents.

In the following chapters, we will delve deeper into the world of political strategy, exploring proven methods and techniques to help you achieve success in your political endeavors. Together, we will lay the groundwork for a fulfilling and impactful career in politics and public service. So, let's embark on this journey, and may the art of winning guide you every step of the way.

POLITICAL CAMPAIGNS AND POLITICAL CAMPAIGN STRATEGIES

Political campaigning represents a complex, yet integral, component of the democratic process in the United States, necessitating meticulous planning and a cohesive strategy. In the forthcoming discussion, we will delve into the diverse landscape of campaign strategies, examining their historical application and effectiveness.

Political Campaigns Unveiled
With the arrival of autumn, the air grows crisp, and the leaves adorn the trees in a delicate mosaic of shifting hues. This season ushers in more than just a change in the natural world; it also marks the onset of a unique spectacle - election season. Every four years, the U.S. enters a period of fervent political activity as presidential candidates unveil their innovative campaign strategies, all with the aim of securing the most esteemed political office in the nation - the presidency.

However, the election fervor isn't limited to this quadrennial event. The interval between these presidential elections also offers a fascinating glimpse into the campaigning methods of senators, representatives, state governors, and legislators.

In the intricate dance of American democracy, campaigning emerges as an inherent privilege and responsibility for republican citizens. It embodies an exercise in democracy, a contest of wit and charm, and to some, it is a riveting spectator sport.

The way candidates conduct their campaigns offers profound insights into their underlying ideals and policy positions. Furthermore, the campaign's tone often predicts the approach they will adopt during their tenure in office. Beyond its substantial political implications, the campaign season also serves as a rich source of riveting television content.

Campaign Settings
There exists a diverse range of campaign strategies in American history, almost as diverse as the number of political candidates themselves. As I outline specifics in terms of political campaigns and the strategies best known for success, it's helpful to understand that these strategies, especially those surviving today, are directly linked to their historic periods with many having evolved from something else. A significant factor to consider is the geographical location of the campaign. Contemporary candidates usually traverse the country (or their respective states for local elections), striving to bring their concerns to the electorate. However, this has not always been the norm.

Historically, many candidates used to on what's known as 'front porch campaigns,' where interested parties, such as newspaper representatives, investors, or supporters, visited the candidate. This approach, which was prevalent in the 19th century, gained notable prominence during the 1896 presidential election. William McKinley, the candidate, spent the majority of his campaign literally on his front porch, while his competitor journeyed hundreds of miles across the country. McKinley's victory underscored the effectiveness of this approach. In contemporary politics, the term 'front porch campaign' is often used to describe a low-budget or minimal-effort campaign, generally signaling an unchallenged or sure-win candidate.

Candidate-Centric Campaigns

Another prevalent strategy involves concentrating on the candidates themselves, rather than the issues at hand. Despite its prominence in modern political discourse, this approach has a long history. In America, instances of focusing on candidates over issues can be traced back to the 1796 election, when opponents critiqued Thomas Jefferson for his fondness for French culture, while John Adams was portrayed as a British Crown sympathizer. This took place during the nation's second real election, after George Washington transitioned between terms without any opposition, highlighting the deep-rooted nature of this approach.

Currently, two primary campaign strategies prioritize candidates over issues. A positive campaign spotlights the candidate's virtues, highlighting their background, experience, and commendable attributes. In contrast, a negative campaign underscores the undesirable traits of the opposing candidate. While sometimes this negativity relates to policy issues (e.g., the candidate's inadequate economic policy), it often devolves into personal attacks or 'mudslinging.' For example, by the 1800 election, opponents were labeling John Adams as a 'repulsive pedant' with a 'hideous hermaphroditic character,' while Thomas Jefferson was accused of endorsing robbery, adultery, and incest. Such is the harsh reality of political mudslinging.

Voter-Centric Campaigns

The final campaign category we'll explore, which has gained significant relevance in the era of digital analytics, is the voter-centric campaign. Essentially, this approach requires candidates to align their campaigns with the concerns that matter most to the voters.

The concept of the 'median voter theorem' encapsulates a

substantial part of this strategy. Under the assumption that voters are more likely to back a candidate whose views align closely with their own, candidates can increase their chances of victory by prioritizing issues that resonate with median voters. These voters are statistically positioned in the middle of the political spectrum, balancing between the two extremes.

Another tactical approach involves 'issue ownership,' suggesting that each political party has a perceived competence in handling specific issues over others. For instance, Republicans often hold greater credibility in matters concerning taxation, while Democrats are usually trusted more on social welfare issues. To win elections, candidates may frame voter concerns in the context of issues that their party is perceived to 'own'.

Another common strategy involves focusing on motivating specific demographics to vote. Two predominant techniques include the 'Bush model,' named after the campaigning methods of President George W. Bush, and the 'Clinton model.' The former targets individuals who already identify with a political party and leverages partisan rivalry to spur them to vote. In contrast, the Clinton model concentrates on persuadable voters, who are yet to commit to a single party, engaging them with popular and centrist issues. Both strategies have demonstrated success in different contexts. Ultimately, the most effective campaign is one that is tailored to the zeitgeist and the individual candidate's appeal.

YOUR POLITICAL PASSION

Politics is not just a profession; it is a calling. It is a calling that requires passion, commitment, and a deep desire to make a positive impact in the world. And if you're reading this book, chances are that you have already felt the pull towards this calling.

Perhaps you're like me, someone who got involved in politics at a young age, passing out campaign materials for a local state senator. Or maybe you're just starting to explore the idea of entering public service, drawn in by the recent political climate or a desire to make a difference.

Regardless of where you are on your political journey, the first step is to find your passion. This can be a daunting task, but it is essential to success in politics.

The first question to ask yourself is: *what issues matter most to me? Do you care deeply about education reform, environmental policy, or social justice? Or do you have a passion for economic development, healthcare, or foreign affairs?* Whatever your passions are, they will be the driving force behind your political career.

Once you have identified your passions, it is important to immerse yourself in the world of politics. Attend local meetings, volunteer for campaigns, and get to know the people who are making a difference in your community. This will not only give you a better understanding of the political process, but it will also help you build a network of like-minded individuals who can support and guide you on your journey.

It is also important to stay informed about current events and political issues. Read newspapers, watch the news, and follow political blogs and social media accounts. This will help you stay up-to-date on the latest developments in your field and prepare you for discussions and debates with others.

Remember that politics is not a one-size-fits-all career. There are many different paths you can take, from working for a political campaign or advocacy organization to running for office yourself. The key is to find what works best for you and your passions.

In the pages that follow, we will explore the many different aspects of a career in politics, from running for office to working behind the scenes. By the end of this book, you will have a better understanding of what it takes to succeed in this field and the tools you need to make your mark on the world. So, let's get started!

CAMPAIGN PLANNING: YOUR OPENING PLAY

Launching a political campaign can feel like gearing up for a high-stakes game, full of excitement and unpredictability. With the right coaching and pre-game strategy, you can not only navigate the complex playbook of politics but also take command of the game's direction. This guide aims to serve as your coach and playbook, arming you with the tools and knowledge to anticipate your opponent's moves and be match-ready.

Just like the turf condition influences the game, the political landscape plays a significant role in any campaign. However, the team's internal dynamics, much like in sports, often become the most crucial determinants of victory or defeat.

Here are 3 types of political campaigns that are like teams destined to lose from internal shortcomings:

1. The campaign that is like a team with a weak game plan and no clear strategy. Lacking direction from the outset, this type of campaign spirals downwards further as the game clock ticks on.
2. The campaign that resembles a team with a strong game plan and strategy but no actionable tactics for scoring. These campaigns waste their resources and drift aimlessly towards the final whistle, constantly on

defense rather than pushing their own offensive.
3. The campaign that is akin to a team that has a clear game plan, strategy, and tactics but fails to execute on the field. This complacent team overlooks the intense training required to win and ultimately falls back on excuses when the scoreboard doesn't favor them.

A championship-winning political campaign is one that meticulously strategizes, develops a compelling game plan, and consistently follows a well-thought-out tactic to engage with voters. This guide is designed to help political teams and candidates achieve this level of success. Just like a playbook, read through it entirely for an overview of the game, then work through it step by step, completing all drills and worksheets to lay a solid groundwork for your campaign strategy.

A written campaign strategy, akin to a playbook for a championship game, outlines the overall political landscape, game plan, and resources needed to reach the final whistle - Election Day. Review the playbook regularly for direction and to track progress. Without a playbook, a campaign is prone to committing costly fouls and ending up on the losing side.

While each campaign is unique, certain fundamental principles, like the rules of a sport, apply universally. This guide will help you adapt these principles to your specific campaign. The essence of any election campaign is simple: communicate a persuasive game plan to potential voters, just like a coach rallying their team. This "golden rule" of politics forms the foundation of any successful campaign - the first half of this book will serve as a coach, guiding you to successfully plan your campaign. The second half will contain play-by-play details and specific instructions, both of which can be selectively referenced; however, I strongly recommend reading the full playbook first and then using the materials for revision or refresher as you push forward.

Whichever method works best for you, I hope you enjoy learning from my decades of first-hand experience in the locker rooms of power, and when you're celebrating your win on election night; I hope you remember the chapters on sportsmanship and responsibility, choosing the high road over a quick win whenever both are in conflict. Game on!

YOUR POLITICAL CAMPAIGN PLAYBOOK: THE WINNING GAME PLAN

Kicking off a campaign might feel like you're trying to catch a Hail Mary pass without even knowing the playbook. I still have vivid recollections of my first solo plays on the political field, and whether you're a rookie candidate or a fresh-off-the-bench campaign manager, the initial blitz can certainly get quite overwhelming if you let it. Information hurtles at you like a well-thrown spiral. Decisions feel like high stakes plays, demanding immediate action. You feel a compelling urgency to address every facet of the campaign NOW, as if you're already in the final quarter.

Take a moment, huddle up, and remember: the campaign is a season-long championship, not just a single game. To kick off, focus on managing these key plays:

- Drafting your campaign game plan or team culture
- Establishing basic administrative plays and processes
- Sketching out an initial budget and fundraising strategy, ensuring you're making the needed yardage

- Setting up your initial digital fan base

- Building effective recruitment and retention strategies for your volunteer squad

- Signing on your coaching staff, advisors, and expert consultants

In the rapidly evolving world of politics, where the course of history can be altered by a single decision or a well-timed speech, the need for practical and adaptable strategies is more crucial than ever. The Political Campaign Playbook is meant to serve as a comprehensive guide that draws upon the collective wisdom of seasoned political professionals, cutting-edge social science research, and real-world experiences to provide an unparalleled blueprint for success in politics, government, and elections.

By the end of this book, you will have gained a deeper understanding of the art and science of modern political strategy, as well as the tools and techniques needed to thrive in the complex world of politics and government. With this knowledge in hand, you will be well-equipped to make a meaningful impact on the world around you and leave a legacy in the annals of history. Welcome to the exhilarating journey of political mastery.

BUILDING YOUR POLITICAL NETWORK AND MANAGING RELATIONSHIPS

Networking is a crucial part of building a successful career in politics. It's not just about knowing the right people, but also about cultivating meaningful relationships and building a supportive community. Review these tips for building a strong network in politics:

Attend events and conferences: Attend political events, conferences, and fundraisers to meet other professionals in the field. This is a great way to build relationships and stay up-to-date on the latest trends and issues in politics.

Join professional organizations: Joining professional organizations, such as political parties, advocacy groups, and trade associations, can help you connect with others in your field and stay involved in the political community.

Volunteer on political campaigns: Volunteering on political campaigns can provide valuable networking opportunities, as well as hands-on experience in the field. You'll have the chance to work alongside other professionals and build relationships with campaign staff and volunteers.

Use social media: Social media can be a powerful tool for building a network in politics. Connect with other professionals on LinkedIn, Twitter, and other platforms, and use these networks to share your own ideas and perspectives.

Cultivate relationships: Building a strong network is not just about making connections, but also about cultivating meaningful relationships over time. Take the time to follow up with contacts, engage in conversations, and offer your own support and resources when possible.

By building a strong network in politics, you can access new opportunities, gain valuable insights and perspectives, and build a supportive community that can help you navigate the challenges of a career in politics. Remember that networking is an ongoing process, and that the relationships you build today can pay off in the future.

The backbone of a thriving political career is an extensive and robust network. As an aspirant for public office, campaign team member, or a government official, you must nurture a vast array of relationships. This spectrum encompasses constituents, donors, fellow politicians, and interest groups.

Your constituents form the cornerstone of your political network. They hold the power to sway electoral outcomes, making it imperative to forge sincere and lasting bonds with them. This involves active listening to their concerns, consistent engagement on social media platforms, and a prompt response to their needs.

Financing is the lifeblood of any campaign, and hence, cultivating relationships with donors is an indispensable part of your political network. Campaigns often come with a hefty price tag, and transparent communication about your fundraising goals and objectives is key to securing financial support.

Equally crucial to your political network are connections with fellow politicians. Whether you're campaigning for a position or already serving in an official capacity, collaboration with other politicians is often required to achieve your objectives. This necessitates fostering relationships that transcend party lines and identifying shared concerns that can serve as a common ground.

Engagement with interest groups and advocacy organizations can be a powerful addition to your political network. These entities can provide robust support and resources, enabling you to realize your political ambitions. Genuine, transparent interaction is the cornerstone of these relationships, coupled with a clear articulation of your priorities and objectives.

The management of these relationships can be a complex task, but a few key strategies can aid the process. Authenticity is paramount: trust and rapport are not built overnight, but with consistent, genuine interaction, they form the bedrock of long-term success. Responsiveness to the needs of your network, from answering constituent queries to finding common ground with fellow politicians, is crucial. Lastly, transparency and honesty are the pillars of any relationship. Admitting errors or acknowledging mistakes can foster respect and strengthen relationships.

Remember, a robust political network is built on the foundation of authenticity, responsiveness, and transparency. It involves a broad array of relationships - with constituents, donors, fellow politicians, and interest groups. A strong network can provide the support and resources necessary to navigate the political landscape successfully and realize your ambitions.

THE SPIRIT OF YOUR TEAM

The Spirit of Your Campaign. Its Essence.
As you experience campaigns on a more frequent basis, it'll be easy to understand the concept that every campaign has an essence or culture that formed, shaped, and uniquely associated with it – many call it a 'culture'. It's the way that staff and volunteers engage with each other and with your opponent and their staff. The challenge is taking the time and creating the space to develop that culture deliberately with your candidate and staff.

Take a few minutes early in the campaign to think through when and how you will engage your new team in conversation around the values they share that brought them to the campaign, and the values and experiences that inform the way they want to work together. One way to do this is to have a meeting very early on explicitly for that purpose, where your team gets to know each other's stories and spends time articulating a few key principles they agree to live by. For example, on the Obama campaign in 2008 the mantra "Respect. Empower. Include." developed by Paul Tewes and his staff in Iowa became the guiding principles of the campaign.

Discuss together, how will staff treat each other? How will they treat the candidate and vice versa? How will you all treat your opponent and their staff when you see them or engage with them?

It's important that you have a team conversation to create agreements or norms that the team feels responsibility for generating and to which they can then be held accountable.

Create a culture of accountability, not rules.
Every campaign has a few core rules for staff. However, it will be impossible for you to create enough rules to manage all of the people you need to engage in your campaign to win. Think about how to create a culture where staff and volunteers are trained to hold each other accountable to achieving performance outcomes, but also to hold each other accountable to the values that bring them together. What training or role playing would that sort of accountability require? Creating this culture early on through role playing and coaching can minimize drama down the road when difficult situations arise.

Create a culture of excellence.
Strong campaigns are those where staff and volunteers are committed not just to the candidate, but also to each other in a common purpose to win. A culture of excellence isn't one that demands instantaneous excellence, or one that threatens to publicly humiliate poor performance for the sake of exercising power.

A culture of excellence is one built on transparency of goals and progress to goals, where staff and volunteers have ownership over and responsibility for key outcomes. With clarity of goals and feedback loops on progress to those goals, your team will lean in, drive themselves and strive for more.

That culture is not possible in a campaign based on fear of embarrassment or fear to admit failure. It only thrives in a context where you as the Manager have created daily and weekly opportunities to evaluate outcomes together, to understand who's doing well and why, who's struggling and why, to help each other problem solve, and to recommit striving for excellence together.

It's the difference between having everyone get on a conference call just to report numbers and having them report transparently so everyone can see in a Google spreadsheet or other online format, then using the call to analyze the outcomes on that spreadsheet together.

Create a culture of learning.
Your entire team—candidate, consultants, staff, and volunteers will not know at the beginning of the campaign what they'll need to know at the end. Whatever experience they've had on campaigns is useful information, but this campaign is new, will face new opportunities and new challenges, and it will only be weathered with a strong commitment to learning and improving over time.

How will you get coached? By whom? How will you set up clear coaching structures across your campaign? How will you reward learning and improvement over time?

Prepare yourself not to complain about your staff, but to ask, "if they're failing, what have I done wrong?" And "What support or conditions would change their outcomes?"

FORGING YOUR GAME PLAN WITH THE CANDIDATE

Getting started can feel overwhelming. You're building the game plan as the clock is ticking. Amid this flurry of activity, one crucial aspect of any campaign can easily be overlooked—the development of trust between the campaign manager and the candidate.

You have a lot to manage staff, advisors, consultants, a future appointee, a budget, and more. However, it is essential to establish and nurture trust between the candidate and the campaign executive, regardless of the role you occupy. Campaign managers should always remember that it's the candidate's campaign, but they are the ones running it. Candidates should regularly acknowledge the intensity and commitment required to operate in such an environment, recognizing that the campaign executive or manager is indispensable for achieving victory.

Formulating Accountability Expectations: Both managers and candidates must hold each other accountable. Did the candidate meet their call time pledge goal for the week? Is the campaign meeting its field goals? Establish a system of regular check-ins to ensure consistent communication and alignment between you and your candidate.

Know What the Other Needs to Know and Give It to Them:

Whether it's reviewing an ad, gaining final approval on television ad spots, or sharing and reviewing budgetary items, establish a decision-making process that outlines which matters require shared review and which can proceed without the other party's final say. Find a system that works effectively for both of you, ensuring a healthy and efficient flow of information.

Know the Inner Circles: Identify the individuals whom your candidate trusts. Build relationships with their close friends, regular campaign communicators, and trusted consultants. Understand their visions for the campaign and share your direction. This way, when you need someone to advocate for a specific action you want your candidate to take, you won't always be the one making the request.

Take a Breath and Count to Ten: It's no secret that disagreements and heated arguments can arise between the candidate and campaign manager. Working in a high-stress, fast-paced, high-stakes environment where one misstep can jeopardize the entire venture, clashes are to be expected. It's crucial to give yourself a moment to calm down, choose your battles wisely, and make your case effectively. If it takes writing a policy paper to increase call time hours, do what it takes to win. Reflecting on the larger impact of the campaign's success can help provide perspective.

Delegate Tasks: Delegating responsibilities is essential to ensure efficient operations and prevent burnout. Divide the workload, leveraging the strengths of various team members to propel the campaign forward. If you're unable to hire more staff, consider recruiting full-time volunteer assistants or scheduling part-time volunteer office assistants. Political science majors at local colleges can be excellent candidates. Even if you're the only paid staffer, there are tasks you should immediately delegate, such as answering phones, collecting news clips, and greeting visitors.

Establish Specific Roles: Identify key roles, such as the campaign attorney and treasurer, early on. Choose individuals who not only have a close relationship with the candidate but also possess a strong understanding of the legal intricacies associated with your campaign's level—whether it's federal, state, or local.

Once these roles are filled, ensure that all legal documents are reviewed by the relevant experts before submission. This will help you navigate the complex legal landscape and avoid potential pitfalls. Additionally, managing financial aspects, such as payroll and tax matters, is crucial. Consider engaging a certified accountant or professional financial service to ensure a smooth financial operation, allowing you to focus on other strategic aspects of the campaign.

Make It Official
- File a statement of organization with the appropriate election division depending on the level of your race (Federal Election Commission, Secretary of State, etc.).
- Open the campaign checking account.
- Get a post office box.
- Get internet and a telephone number. Your campaign's number should <u>never</u> be the candidate's or your own personal mobile phone number.
- Find and rent an office. The office should <u>not</u> be in the candidate's home.
- Inventory the resources you have access to - computers, desks, printers, office supplies, and copiers.
- Create a form explaining the laws governing in-kind contributions for your race and asking for the donor information needed for those who make in-kind contributions.
- Make a list of the office furniture, equipment, and supplies that you will need (computers, desks, printers, office supplies, copiers) and start soliciting those in-kind contributions.
- Make a short list of the essential early needs of the campaign that you can't get through in-kind donations. BE CONSERVATIVE! Money spent now is money you won't have at the end of the race to run that

last TV ad.

After Its Figured Out. Finalize It as Policy or System.

Establish robust administrative structures to effectively manage the inherent unpredictability of a campaign. These structures will streamline incoming data and regulate the allocation of resources.

Financial Management: Choose an appropriate financial management system to track potential donors, record pledges, and contributions, and generate financial reports. Initially, this could be as simple as using spreadsheets, especially if funds are limited. Maintain a clear record of all financial transactions, including photocopies of every check received, along with any accompanying materials. Ensure all banking information, deposit slips, and receipts are securely filed and easily accessible.

Communications Management: Work closely with your candidate to establish a clear approval process for all public communications, including website content, press releases, and other external communications materials. Determine who holds the final authority for signoffs, who is authorized to interact with the media, and who should refrain from doing so.

Scheduling Coordination: Devise a system to manage scheduling requests. Establish clear communication channels with the candidate to coordinate schedules before making any commitments. Have a plan in place for politely deferring or declining scheduling requests. If the candidate has a scheduler in another government office, company, or organization, define their role in coordination with campaign staff. Set firm ground rules regarding changes to important campaign times, like call time, to ensure they are not subject to alteration by external individuals.

PRE-GAME: PREPARATION AND PLANNING

The actual planning is far more complex than adhering to a single rule. This manual will guide you through a systematic process of creating a written campaign plan, including:

1. Conducting research to prepare for the campaign.
2. Establishing a strategic campaign goal based on the number of votes needed to win.
3. Analyzing and targeting voters.
4. Developing a campaign message.
5. Devising a voter contact plan.
6. Implementing the plan.

While this manual cannot provide solutions to every problem your campaign will encounter, nor dictate your message or identify your supporters, it can supply the framework to help you think strategically and methodically.

The candidate, campaign manager, and key advisors should collaborate in a strategic planning meeting, working through this manual rigorously and producing a written campaign plan. A written plan ensures that everyone is on the same page and prevents the campaign from drifting aimlessly. *If it's not written down, there is no plan.*

Once the plan is in place, adhere to it with discipline. While campaigns must remain adaptable to changing circumstances, any deviations should be carefully considered considering the original research and strategy.

A political campaign is an intense and demanding experience, requiring dedication and hard work. However, it can also be exhilarating, rewarding, and enjoyable. To the campaign workers, your contributions to the democratic process are commendable. To the candidates, your willingness to serve your community and participate in democracy is praiseworthy.

ANALYZING THE FIELD: UNDERSTANGING YOUR POLITICAL LANDSCAPE

Every political campaign is distinct, with its own set of challenges and opportunities. Recognizing these differences and the context in which your campaign will unfold is vital for success. To better comprehend your unique situation, you must first thoroughly research your political landscape. This will enable you to develop a tailored, effective strategy that accounts for the specific circumstances of your campaign.

Start by analyzing the election type and rules, the characteristics of the district and voters, past election results, and key factors influencing the current election. Additionally, assess the strengths and weaknesses of your candidate and the viable opponents. While some answers may be immediately apparent, others may require diligent research or educated guesses.
To streamline the research process, consider delegating different sections to members of your campaign team. Establish a time limit to ensure the information gathered is used effectively in crafting your strategy. Depending on your resources and

campaign size, you may also explore more scientific research methods such as political polling or focus groups.

Gain a comprehensive understanding of the election rules, district demographics, political landscape, voter behavior, past election outcomes, and factors affecting the current election. This information will help you better target your message and develop a strategic approach to winning the election.

It's also essential to objectively evaluate your candidate and opponents to identify strengths and weaknesses. By doing so, you can better anticipate potential challenges and opportunities, as well as craft a more compelling message. Be thorough and organized with your opposition research, documenting sources and maintaining a system for easy access to the information.

Once you've gathered and analyzed all pertinent data, compile it into an organized notebook and draft a summary to serve as the foundation for your campaign strategy and plan. By carefully considering the unique factors influencing your campaign, you'll be better equipped to develop a winning strategy that resonates with your target audience.

POLITICAL THEORY AND IDEOLOGY IN AMERICAN POLITICS

The Theory and Philosophy

Although I've designed this book to be used by first time-candidates or young people who are soon-to-be-candidates or political operatives – regardless of who you might be, it'll always be helpful for you to have a basic understanding of the core concepts that have essentially built our basic political theories here in the U.S. I encourage you to continue to educate yourself in this area but let's be honest here: I'm going to provide you with just enough information to allow you to be perceived as an expert on the subject while not providing a single fact or insight beyond. Accordingly, to understand American politics, one must first delve into the roots of political theory and the work of philosophers who have shaped its foundation. The American experiment, as it is often called, was heavily influenced by the ideas of European philosophers, particularly John Locke and Thomas Hobbes. These two thinkers had opposing views on the nature of human beings, the role of government, and the extent of individual rights.

John Locke, an English philosopher from the Enlightenment era, believed that humans are born with natural rights to life, liberty, and property. He argued that governments are formed to protect these rights and that they derive their power from the consent of the governed. If a government fails to protect these rights or becomes tyrannical, the people have the right to revolt and establish a new government. Locke's ideas are deeply ingrained in American political thought, as evidenced by the Declaration of Independence, which echoes his views on natural rights and the consent of the governed.

In contrast, Thomas Hobbes, another English philosopher, had a more pessimistic view of human nature. He believed that humans are naturally selfish and prone to violence, requiring a strong, centralized authority to maintain order and prevent society from descending into chaos. Hobbes famously wrote that life without government would be "solitary, poor, nasty, brutish, and short." His ideas laid the groundwork for the concept of the social contract, which posits that people willingly give up some of their freedoms in exchange for protection and order from the government.

Political Ideologies in America

Political ideologies, while increasingly visible in the age of social media, have been integral to human society since its inception, guiding the collective thought processes of diverse groups. So, let's delve into what constitutes a political ideology.

Political ideologies encompass coherent, interconnected beliefs about political theory and social policy. A defining characteristic of these ideologies is their ability to provide a cohesive framework for beliefs within their realm, enabling individuals who identify with a particular ideology to envision their version of an ideal society and work towards it.

Tracing the Origins of Ideology

Comprehending political ideologies is critical, given the significant role they play in shaping policy development. In a vibrant political landscape, myriad parties compete to see their preferred policies actualized within established governance structures. This leads to the question: how did this mode of governance come into existence, or more specifically, what are the origins of ideology?

The term 'ideology' emerged in the 18th century, crafted by A.L.C. Destutt de Tracy to refer to the science of ideas. The term's etymology harks back to the Greek word 'ideo-', denoting form or pattern. This is fitting, given that an ideology categorizes various aspects of the world within a distinct form or framework. An ideology must be expansive enough to encompass a broad range of political theories, while maintaining its distinctiveness and differentiating itself from other ideologies. For instance, an ideology advocating power concentration in the hands of the state cannot simultaneously espouse the empowerment of the general populace. Instead, the ideology in question must maintain consistency, interpreting all aspects of political theory through the lens of state-centric power distribution. American politics has been influenced by several ideological currents, which can be broadly categorized into conservatism, neo-conservatism, liberalism, and neo-liberalism. These ideologies are not mutually exclusive and have evolved over time, often overlapping, or borrowing ideas from one another.

Political ideologies represent collective or individual belief systems concerning political theory and social policy. Given the variety of perspectives on societal functioning, numerous political ideologies have emerged. Below are some of the major political ideologies and the core beliefs they uphold.

Liberalism - Regarded as the prevailing ideology in the United States, Liberalism champions individual rights, freedom of speech, and democracy. Generally, liberals uphold capitalism and individual choice, recognizing the necessity of government but advocating for its limitation.

Socialism - Focusing primarily on distribution and production, Socialism advocates for communal sharing of goods and services. It also supports extensive social programs and harmonization with democratic governance or the development of accountable, open institutions. Notably, socialism shares a commonality with liberalism in advocating equality before the law. Cooperation is a pivotal value in this ideology.

Fascism - Fascist ideology supports an authoritarian government and suppresses dissenting viewpoints. It stands in stark contrast to liberal ideologies.

Conservatism - Conservatives value free enterprise and respect traditional institutions and beliefs, often underpinned by religious rationale. Advocating for private ownership of goods and services, conservatives favor stability and continuity over drastic governmental changes.

Progressivism - Progressives argue for the vital role of government in initiating social reform and economic enhancement for everyday citizens.

Communism - Largely attributed to Karl Marx, Communism strives for class equality. Within the Marxist framework, all property is government-owned, and individuals are compensated according to their abilities. Often, it is regarded as an evolved form of socialism.

Most political ideologies share similar values and beliefs.

Political Party Associations in the United States

In the U.S., political parties often align with political ideologies. For instance, the Republican Party is typically more associated with Conservatism compared to the Democratic Party.

Defining Political Views

Political views refer to individual opinions on specific political matters. These views are significantly shaped by political ideologies, guiding the direction and intensity of an individual's political leanings. For instance, a liberal is prone to endorse views consistent with free speech, while a fascist may lean towards suppressing dissenting voices. Political views, in their totality, constitute the overarching ideology.

The Formation of Political Views

The formation of political views is profoundly influenced by one's world view, which can be shaped by personal characteristics and experiences. Studies in psychology suggest a correlation between liberal viewpoints and the personality trait known as openness to experience. This correlation aligns well with liberal values that emphasize openness to different perspectives and freedom of speech. Conversely, the conservative viewpoint, known for adhering to time-tested principles, may be more attractive to religious individuals given its resistance to radical changes in social policies, mirroring religious doctrines that resist alterations.

The Significance of Political Ideologies

Political ideologies play a crucial role in shaping cohesive societies. A collective, agreed-upon value system can guide a government towards unifying decisions, foster a sense of identity among citizens, and stimulate action. Historically, ideological cohesion has often been the determining factor between a society succumbing to external forces or successfully defending its territories. However, the unifying force of political ideologies also harbors the potential for manipulation and control, given the potency of shared belief systems.

The Current State of Political Affairs

The current state of American politics is characterized by increasing polarization and ideological entrenchment. Both major political parties, the Democrats and the Republicans, have moved further to the left and right of the political spectrum, respectively. This has resulted in a decline in bipartisanship and a rise in political tribalism. This has created an environment where compromise and pragmatic solutions are often seen as betrayals of core principles, further exacerbating the divide between the two parties.

In this climate, more extreme voices have gained prominence, and the political center has been increasingly marginalized. Social media and the 24-hour news cycle have further contributed to this polarization, as politicians and voters are exposed to echo chambers that reinforce their pre-existing beliefs and demonize those who hold opposing views.

However, it is crucial to recognize that American politics is not static. It has always been marked by periods of ideological realignment and shifting coalitions. In the face of these challenges, there remains a strong demand for politicians who can bridge the divide and find common ground on critical issues.

This book is meant to equip you and all aspiring public servants, candidates, and political practitioners with the knowledge and tools to navigate this complex landscape. By understanding the foundations of political theory and ideology, as well as the current state of American politics, everyone will be better prepared to develop effective strategies and forge lasting connections with voters across the ideological spectrum. I firmly believe that armed with this knowledge, each of those who aspire to enter public service or work in politics and government can make a meaningful impact on the American political landscape, helping to heal divisions and work towards a more united, prosperous future for all citizens.

DEFINING A WINNING STRATEGY

Victory in any political campaign hinges on setting clear goals and strategically allocating resources. Many campaigns lose focus, failing to calculate the precise number of votes needed to secure a win and identify the sources of these votes. In this step, we will streamline the process by narrowing down the target audience, leveraging research and informed predictions.

1. **Determine your district's total population:** This includes everyone residing in your district, not just eligible voters. This figure should be larger than the total number of voters, as it encompasses non-registered residents and minors.

2. **Identify the total number of eligible voters:** This refers to all registered voters in the district who could potentially cast a vote in the upcoming election.

3. **Predict voter turnout:** Estimate the number of expected votes based on previous elections. Factors such as changes in political climate or significant events may impact turnout, so adjust your predictions accordingly.

4. **Calculate the votes needed to win:** This number will vary based on the number of candidates and the electoral system. For a simple majority, you'll need 50% of the

votes plus one. Consider being conservative in your estimates to avoid underestimating the votes needed.

5. **Estimate the number of households these voters belong to:** Assuming that each household has an average of two voters, you can reduce the number of individuals you need to communicate with. Keep in mind that members of the same household may vote similarly, though this is not always the case.

CAMPAIGN STRATEGY

Complete this form with information to build your custom campaign strategy

District's Total Population _____

District's Eligible Voters _____

Number of Votes Cast in Previous Election _____

Number of Votes Cast in Election Before (2 Elections Ago) _____

$+ \div 2 =$ _____ $+ 1 =$ **Win Number**

Expected Turnout

Expected Turnout $\times .52 =$ **Vote Goal**

% of Voters Expected to Vote _____

Votes Calculated from % _____

Compare to Expected Turnout number listed above and adjust as needed. Its better to estimate slightly high than slightly low.

How many candidates are running? _____

# of candidates that are serious contenders _____

If the election were held today, what percentage of the vote would each candidate receive?

1. _____
2. _____
3. _____

On average, how many voters live in one household?

Do voters in the same household typically vote for the same candidate?

How many households must you secure support from to guarantee victory?

Out of every ten voters you speak to, how many can you persuade to vote for you?

How many households must you communicate with to reach enough voters to achieve victory?

Notes: _____

WORKSHEET 2: DEFINING A WINNING STRATEGY

Using your research and best judgment, answer the following questions and incorporate them into your campaign plan:

1. What is your district's total population?
2. How many eligible voters reside in your district?
3. What percentage of these voters do you expect to vote in this election?
4. How many votes does this translate to?
5. How many candidates are running for this position?
6. How many of these candidates are serious contenders?
7. If the election were held today, what percentage of the vote would each candidate receive?
8. What percentage of votes cast is needed to win?
9. How many votes (in real numbers) are needed to win?
10. On average, how many voters live in one household?
11. Do voters in the same household typically vote for the same candidate?
12. How many households must you secure support from to guarantee victory?
13. Out of every ten voters you speak to, how many can you persuade to vote for you?
14. How many households must you communicate with to reach enough voters to achieve victory?

OFFENSIVE PLAYS: DEVELOPING YOUR MESSAGE

UNDERSTANDING THE MESSAGE

Once you've identified your target audience, the next step is to craft a powerful and persuasive message that resonates with them. This message conveys the reasons behind your candidacy and why voters should choose you over your opponents. Although it may seem straightforward, creating an effective campaign message is a complex process.

To clarify, a campaign message isn't merely a candidate's platform or a list of issues they plan to address. While these elements can contribute to the message, the core of the message should be a clear, consistent statement that is repeated throughout the campaign to sway your target voters.

PRIORITIZING VOTERS' CONCERNS AND INFORMATION SOURCES

Remember that voters have a multitude of concerns and are constantly exposed to various information sources. Your campaign message must break through the noise and effectively capture their attention.

Respect your voters and acknowledge that they can quickly identify insincere messages. To create a persuasive message, consider the following characteristics:

1. **BREVITY:** A concise message is crucial, as voters have little patience for long-winded politicians. If you can't deliver your message in under a minute, you risk losing the voter's attention and potentially their vote.
2. **TRUTHFULNESS AND CREDIBILITY:** Your message should align with your values, background, and policies. Be consistent and avoid making unrealistic promises. To establish credibility, substantiate your claims with evidence of your experience and expertise.
3. **RELEVANCE AND PERSUASIVENESS:** Address topics that matter to your target audience. Discuss issues that directly impact voters' lives, rather than those that are solely significant to public policy. Your goal is to convince voters that you are the best representative for them and earn their vote.
4. **CONTRAST:** Emphasize the differences between you and your opponents to help voters make a clear choice. Illustrate your unique stance on key issues and how it sets you apart from other candidates.
5. **CLARITY AND EMOTIONAL APPEAL:** Use language that voters easily understand and relate to. Speak to their hearts by connecting your message to their core values and the challenges they face daily.
6. **TARGETING:** Tailor your message to your likely supporters, as identified in your voter targeting strategy. Provide clear information about how you represent their interests and avoid generic messages that fail to resonate with anyone.

By incorporating these characteristics, you can create a compelling campaign message that effectively engages your target audience and motivates them to vote for you. Remember that voters deserve a clear understanding of your platform and your intentions, so take the time to craft a message that resonates with them and speaks to their concerns.

ENGAGING WITH VOTERS
HOW STORY WORKS

Stories motivate others by invoking our emotions. Emotions help us connect with others. Emotions inform us of what we value in ourselves, in others, and in the world. Stories enable us to express our values in a motivational way to others. Stories appeal to our hearts, while strategy appeals to our heads. Both are important to successful campaigns.

Some emotions inhibit action, but other emotions facilitate action. Action is inhibited by inertia, fear, self-doubt, isolation, and apathy. Action is facilitated by urgency, hope, solidarity, and anger. Organizers use stories that convey urgency and hope to make people feel like they can make a difference and create change. These stories are effective because we can identify with the character in the story.

Stories convey the values of the storyteller when we know the challenges they faced, the choices they made in response to those challenges, and the outcomes of those choices.

Ask

All of us have faced challenges throughout our lives. In many ways, these challenges define who we are as individuals. The key focus in our personal stories is the time when we faced a challenge or challenges, and we came to a critical moment of choice. A point in our lives when we had to choose in the face of uncertainty or difficulty, and the decision shaped the values we have today. The outcome of the story gives us hope. Because we can empathetically identify with the person in the story, we feel their courage; we become connected to that person, are inspired by them, and moved to action.

Think about times you were moved to action and why. When did you: First care about making your voice heard? Develop a concern for others? Come to care about abuses of power? About poverty? About the world? Why? When did you feel you had to do something about it? Why did you feel you could? What were the circumstances? What was the outcome?

Your story is most powerful when it is connected to the story of the Democratic campaign, the community you are building, and the action you wish others to take.

Just as with a person, communities face challenges and they have to make choices that will ultimately decide their outcomes. Your story should communicate why our community, organization, and movement have been called on to support Democratic candidates and their plan for a better future, particularly in the context of Oklahoma campaigns.

In the end, your story also needs to move people to specific action by painting a detailed picture of how things might be different if we act, giving us the hope that if we act now we can make a difference.

The first version of your story should be three minutes in length. Eventually, you will have two versions of your story of different lengths: a three-minute version for one-on-one meetings and house meetings, and a 90-second version for quick introductions or brief encounters. When considering what to cut and what to keep in your story, remember that vivid details and a clear plot are important, but you don't necessarily need each detail of each plot point. Remember to build urgency. Give an introduction that moves into the challenge and choice of your story that transitions into the outcome that is linked to your work with our movement.

PLAYMAKING 101: TELLING YOUR STORY

Everyone has a personal story; in fact, we have many stories. Some are stories of loss and others of hope. Often the stories of loss inform those of hope and serve as motivation to work for a better future.

Reflect on your own personal story. What challenges have you faced? What key choices did you make? How did the choice both shape and convey your values? What brings you to this movement? When did you decide to support Democratic principles? Why? When did you decide to become an Organizer? Why?

Your personal story is not just told in person but over the phones, Twitter, Facebook and official blogs. Sharing your story and the stories of your volunteers as part of the larger grassroots campaign's story online is one of the narratives we can most cleanly and clearly control to drive people to action for our team. This is an important part in creating the face of the grassroots campaign in your community.

What would it look like in the following formats?
Blog: Long format story that focuses on one key piece of your story that connects you to the larger movement. Think about telling your story in a way that doesn't just go from one moment in your life to another but how this one thing or issue has brought you to where you are today. Explain why you are organizing.

Facebook: Your story is not static. Facebook lets you tell an ongoing story of your organizing. It is told in the photos you post, the links you share, and your interaction with your state page, volunteers, and friends.

Tweets: The story of your organizing is also interwoven with others. It's the photos you share, your personal thoughts, quotes of volunteers you re-tweet, and political messaging you share.

YOUR GAMEPLAN – YOUR NARRATIVE

Regardless of the setting that you tell your story in, most stories are best felt by the listener when the storyteller has a specific challenge and choice to their story. Some stories are centered on a specific challenge, but sometimes there are multiple challenges interrelated. Reflect back on challenges you had to face, the choices you made about how to deal with them, and the satisfactions—or frustrations— you experienced.

Narrative: A Potent Tool for Communication
No matter the cultural context, narrative stands as the most potent means of communication. A captivating story does more than relay facts: it connects the narrator's message to familiar narratives, infusing the story with meaning and memorability. It incites emotional responses, compelling people to care, and conveys a moral lesson, which resonates with people's values.

Top-tier political communicators are master storytellers. An effective Engagement Campaign leverages the power of narrative to inspire and mobilize people.

Aspire with the Power of Narrative
The ensuing pyramid illustrates how your campaign should resonate with voters on multiple levels. This applies to every facet of your campaign, from soliciting donations, to crafting press releases, to rallying volunteers. If your appeal is limited to contrasting your stance with your opponent's, or to the issues and

policy level, it may be less challenging but also less effective.

Aspirations and Values

The most potent appeal to people is at the "aspirational" level. At this level, voters see their values and hopes mirrored in your campaign. Voters are most driven to support candidates who embody their own aspirations and values and who they perceive as leading the community towards the future they envision. To stimulate public participation and turnout, your campaign narrative needs to connect with people at an aspirational level.

Social and Emotional Connections

Supporting a candidate or engaging in any campaign action is inherently a social act. When volunteers and voters evaluate a candidate, they are curious about the people involved. This curiosity often remains, even if they don't explicitly inquire about the social facets of a campaign. People assess the personal qualities of the candidate, as well as the candidate's supporters. Voters want to see themselves in the people propelling the campaign. Furthermore, volunteers seek a meaningful social experience – they want to spend time with like-minded individuals. Thus, it's crucial to make your campaign a vibrant, enjoyable, and meaningful place for volunteers.

Contrast and Distinction

Elections are about making choices. It's crucial to draw a vivid contrast with your opponent. However, the comparative aspect of the campaign should extend beyond issue stances. Your candidate's biography, campaign message, and even the aesthetics of your website, advertisements, and events should distinguish you from others.

Issues & Policy

While it's important for voters to know where the candidate stands on key issues, they don't need an exhaustive rundown of the candidate's policies and programs. Many campaigns fall into the trap of trying to engage voters and media in policy details. While policy has its place and can occasionally be pivotal when an event or crisis thrusts a candidate's response into the spotlight, it's worth remembering that it's at the bottom of the motivational hierarchy. Moreover, a candidate can only formulate policy within the framework of governance and negotiation with others. The candidate's core values, which will influence policy negotiation down the line, are most crucial.

Entering the world of politics for the first time can be a daunting task for candidates and campaign managers alike. However, the key to success lies in the ability to craft a compelling political narrative that resonates with voters. This chapter aims to guide first-time candidates and campaign managers on how to develop and communicate a powerful narrative that sets the stage for a successful campaign.

Understanding the Importance of Narrative for First-Time Candidates

For first-time candidates, the task of breaking into the political arena can seem daunting. Amid the complexities of campaigning, understanding policy details, and managing public appearances, the power of a well-crafted narrative often gets overlooked. However, it is this narrative that often proves to be the deciding factor in political races, especially for first-time candidates.

A political narrative is essentially your story. It is a cohesive thread that binds your personal experiences, values, and vision for the future into a compelling story that resonates with your constituents. It goes beyond your political platform and policy proposals. It provides context, offering voters a glimpse into **who you are**, **where you come from**, and **why you are running for office**.

In essence, *your narrative humanizes you*. It makes you relatable and memorable, allowing voters to connect with you on a personal level. This is especially important for first-time candidates who are still relatively unknown to the public. A strong narrative can help you establish credibility, differentiate yourself from other candidates, and build a loyal base of supporters.

The Role of Narrative in Politics: Inspiring Case Studies of First-Time Candidates

Alexandria Ocasio-Cortez: Ocasio-Cortez's story of being a bartender-turned-politician resonated with many working-class Americans. Her narrative of struggle and resilience, coupled with her vision for a more equitable society, allowed her to defeat a ten-term incumbent in the 2018 Democratic primary for New York's 14th congressional district.

Barack Obama: Although not a first-time candidate when he ran for president, Obama's narrative during his 2008 campaign was powerful. His story of being the son of a Kenyan father and a Kansas mother, his experiences growing up, his work as a community organizer, and his vision for change resonated deeply with many Americans, leading him to win the presidency.

Jacinda Ardern: When Ardern became the leader of New Zealand's Labour Party just seven weeks before the general election, she was relatively unknown. However, her authenticity, coupled with her narrative of being a young, progressive woman pushing for change, resonated with voters and led her party to victory.

These case studies underline the power of a well-crafted narrative. They show that a compelling narrative can help first-time candidates connect with voters, build credibility, and ultimately win elections. The key is to ensure that your narrative is authentic, relatable, and weaved seamlessly into your campaign messaging.

Strategic Advice:

- Craft a compelling narrative that resonates with voters on an aspirational level, reflecting their hopes and values.
- Foster a vibrant and meaningful social experience for volunteers and supporters to build a strong community around your campaign.
- Clearly distinguish your campaign from your opponents on multiple levels, from policy positions to personal narratives.
- Prioritize communicating your candidate's core values and broad policy stances over detailed policy proposals.

QUICKPLAY: MASTERING THE ONE-MINUTE STATEMENT

1. Compile a list of reasons why voters should choose your candidate or party.
2. From the list, select the most compelling arguments and craft a concise statement that answers the question "why are you running for office?" or "why should I support you?"
3. Time yourself reading the statement aloud. Ensure it can be delivered in under a minute; if not, trim it down. Remember, voters may not pay attention to an entire speech, so focus on the essentials.
4. Assess the statement based on credibility, relevance to target voters, personal experience, and differentiation from opponents. If needed, remove any unnecessary words or phrases.
5. Refine your statement to perfection, keeping it under a minute. As you use it while interacting with voters, it will continue to improve.

EXERCISE:
Reflections on Life's Key Moments

DIRECTIONS

List 5 Key Moments of Choice From Your Life. What are some moments when you stepped up (or failed to step up) to a challenge? What moments have been defining for your life?

FEEDBACK PROCESS

You will use these moments in the next exercise to begin to build your story.

1.

2.

3.

4.

5.

CHALLENGE, CHOICE, AND OUTCOME:

A good public story is drawn from the series of choices that have structure the "plot" of your life - the challenges you faced, choices you made, and outcomes you experienced.

The plot consists of three components:

- Challenge: Why did you feel it was a challenge? What was so challenging about it? Why was it your challenge?

- Choice: Why did you make the choice you did? Where did you get the courage—or not? Where did you get the hope—or not? How did it feel?

- Outcome: How did the outcome feel? Why did it feel that way? What did it teach you? What do you want to teach us? How do you want us to feel?

EXERCISE:
Reflection, Challenge, Choice, Outcome

DIRECTIONS
Choose three of the key moments of your life from above. As you complete the grid below, continue to ask yourself questions. What choices did you make? Why did you make those choices? Why did you do this and not that? Keep asking yourself why.

FEEDBACK PROCESS
You will use these maps in the next exercise to flesh out the details of your story.

CHALLENGE	CHOICE	OUTCOME

- What did you learn from reflecting on these moments of challenge, choice, and outcome?
- How do they make you feel?
- Do they teach you anything about yourself, about your family, about your peers, your community, your nation, the world you live in—about what really matters to you?

- What about these stories was so intriguing?
- What emotions were conveyed in this story and what values were linked to these emotions?
- Which elements offered real perspective into your own life?

EXERCISE:
Adding Detail and Interest

DAVID D. ROBERTS

DIRECTIONS
Now that you have three story maps from your life, pick the story that best illustrates how and why you chose to be here and add detail to it by answering the following questions.

FEEDBACK PROCESS
You will use these details in the final version of your story that you will share with a small group.

1. What are the particular details that you remember, what did it look like, what did it feel like, what values were conveyed?

2. How did it move you to action?

3. Who would you be telling this story to? What about it would move them?

EXERCISE:
Linking Your Story to the Democratic Story

POLITICAL CAMPAIGN PLAYBOOK

DIRECTIONS
Your story is compelling, has a clear plot, and details to make it vivid. Now link your story explicitly to our movement and turn it into a call to action.

FEEDBACK PROCESS
You will use these details in the final version of your story that you will share with a small group.

1. How are you a part of Obama for America's story?

2. How is Obama for America a part of your story? Past, present, future?

3. Which of President Obama's Accomplishments have impacted you personally?

PRACTICE

Telling your story takes practice. You will have to work constantly to refine and tighten your story as well as adjust your story to certain situations or audiences. As organizers, we are never done with telling our story, so practice will be constant.

Practice in your head, then practice with a partner. Listen to their feedback as to how to make the story even better, but also how the story made them feel. How can you use your story to make an even better connection to your listener?

"During my first two years of college, perhaps because the values my mother had taught me - hard work, honesty, empathy - had resurfaced after a long hibernation; or perhaps because of the example of wonderful teachers and lasting friends, I began to notice a world beyond myself...So that by the time I graduated from college, I was possessed with a crazy idea - that I would work at a grassroots level to bring about change."

- Pres. Barack Obama

NAVIGATING THE INTRICACIES OF YOUR POLITICAL CAMPAIGN

Armed with a comprehensive understanding of your political landscape, you can now begin to navigate the intricacies of your campaign more effectively. By using the research you've conducted as a foundation, tailor your approach to better resonate with your target audience and exploit the opportunities that arise.

1. **Craft a compelling message:** Based on your research, develop a message that addresses the concerns and interests of your constituents. Ensure that your message aligns with your candidate's strengths and sets them apart from the competition. Consider how your message complements the broader narrative of your political party or other candidates on the same ticket.

2. **Build a strong campaign team:** Assemble a dedicated and skilled team that can support your candidate and execute your campaign strategy. Delegate responsibilities based on each team member's strengths and expertise. Maintain open lines of communication and regularly evaluate your team's progress.

3. **Develop a targeted voter outreach plan:** Utilize the demographic data and voter behavior patterns you've gathered to create a targeted outreach plan. This plan should focus on engaging key segments of the electorate, including undecided voters and groups most likely to support your candidate. Prioritize your resources to

maximize your impact on these crucial groups.
4. **Design a comprehensive media strategy**: Leverage your knowledge of local media outlets, reporters, and deadlines to build a robust media strategy. Determine the best channels and methods for disseminating your message and engaging with the press. Stay agile and be prepared to adapt your strategy based on media coverage and public reaction.
5. **Establish a coordinated campaign effort**: Collaborate with other candidates, campaigns, or organizations that share your goals and values. Coordinated efforts can amplify your message, mobilize supporters, and maximize your resources.
6. **Regularly review and adjust your strategy**: As your campaign progresses, continuously evaluate the effectiveness of your strategy and make necessary adjustments. Stay informed about any changes in the political landscape and be prepared to pivot when needed.

By carefully crafting your campaign strategy and staying attuned to the unique factors influencing your race, you'll be well-positioned to connect with your target audience and secure a victory on Election Day.

THE ANATOMY OF THE HARD ASK

Volunteer:
Hi, is this Marshall?

Marshall:
Yes, this is Marshall.

Volunteer:
Marshall, there are only 21 days left until Election Day and **now more than ever it is vital that we all pull together** to guard the change that we fought so hard for over these past few years. Can we count on you to come in and **phone bank with us either at 7pm on Tuesday or 7pm on Wednesday?**

— *Emphasis on being a part of something bigger than the individual*

— *Asks for something specific using Either/Or format*

Marshall:
No, I'm busy.

Volunteer:
Okay, we could really use your help canvassing or entering data with us this weekend if calling isn't your style. Would you like to canvass, phonebank, or enter data?

— *Offer up other opportunities. Don't take "no" for an answer*

Marshall:
Well...I think I like the idea of canvassing best.

Volunteer:
Great! When in the next three days works for you?

Marshall:
My boss keeps me very busy.

— *Be persistent*

Volunteer:
When does work for you?

Marshall:
I guess I could canvass on Sunday

Volunteer:
Great we'll see you on **Sunday at noon for our kick-off canvass.**

— *Specificity is key*

OFFENSIVE TACTIC: CRAFTING THE MESSAGE BOX

The message box is a political strategy that provides a structured approach to building effective messages and countering opponents' claims.

THE MESSAGE BOX

What *we* are saying about *ourselves*.	What *they* are saying about *themselves*.
What *we* are saying about *them*.	What *they* are saying about *us*.

The message box is a critical tool in the arsenal of any political campaign. It's a powerful vehicle for defining your candidate's image, framing the debate, and shaping public opinion. It distills the core messaging strategy into four quadrants, each representing a key aspect of the campaign's narrative and counter-narrative.

What we say about us: This is the heart of your campaign, your candidate's brand. It encapsulates the positive attributes, achievements, and policies of your candidate or party. It's essential to construct a compelling and relatable story that resonates with the target audience. The narrative should be clear, concise, and consistent across all platforms and communications. From public speeches to social media posts, this message should underscore your candidate's unique qualifications, leadership capabilities, and vision for the future.

Remember that voters are not just looking for policies; they're looking for character and connection. Your narrative should evoke emotion and illustrate your candidate's personal commitment to the community and constituents. Humanize your candidate by sharing personal stories and experiences that shaped their life and political journey.

What we say about them: This refers to the critique or contrast with your opponents. It's crucial to maintain a delicate balance here. You want to highlight the differences between your candidate and the opposition without resorting to personal attacks or mudslinging. Stick to policy differences, past voting records, and contrasting visions for the future.

While it might be tempting to exploit an opponent's personal failings, it is generally more effective to focus on their professional shortcomings and policy failures. This approach not only respects the ethical boundaries of political discourse, but it also has a higher chance of swaying undecided or independent voters who are often put off by personal attacks.

What they say about us: Anticipating and addressing the criticisms your opponents will level at your candidate is crucial for effective damage control. Regularly monitor your opponent's public statements, press releases, and social media activity to understand their attack strategy.

Once you have a handle on their approach, you can develop proactive defenses and responses. If possible, turn these criticisms into opportunities to reaffirm your candidate's strengths and commitment. Remember, it's not just about denying or deflecting accusations, but also about reframing the conversation in a way that benefits your campaign.

What they say about them: This quadrant requires you to think from your opponent's perspective. How are they presenting their own attributes and achievements? Understanding their self-portrayal will give you insights into their campaign strategy, target audience, and potential weaknesses.

Stay updated on their public engagements, policy proposals, and campaign promises. This information will allow you to preemptively counter their narrative and even exploit gaps in their messaging or policy platforms. Highlight where your candidate's policies and vision are superior and provide a more beneficial alternative for the electorate.

In conclusion, the message box isn't just a tool for crafting talking points; it's a strategic framework for understanding the political landscape, guiding your campaign's narrative, and effectively countering your opponent's tactics. By systematically addressing each quadrant of the message box, you can ensure your campaign stays proactive, adaptive, and compelling, regardless of the twists and turns of the political journey.

PLAYING DEFENSE: BALANCING CREDIBILITY AND CONTRAST

The ultimate goal of your messaging strategy is to establish higher credibility with target voters than your opponents. This can be achieved through emphasizing your candidate's positive traits and positions on issues, as well as highlighting the shortcomings of your opponents.

ISSUES AND CAMPAIGN MESSAGING
Your campaign message should act as a unifying theme for the various issues that matter to your target audience. Consider the analogy of a tree: your message is the trunk, providing strength and stability, while the branches represent the range of issues addressed, all connected to the central message. Bill Clinton's 1992 presidential campaign and Barack Obama's 2008 campaign are prime examples of how to effectively tie issues to a consistent, resonant message.

STRATEGIC COMMUNICATIONS THROUGHOUT THE CAMPAIGN
As you develop and refine your messaging, it's important to communicate it strategically throughout the campaign. Consistency and repetition are essential to ensuring that your

target audience internalizes and remembers your message. Here are some recommendations to effectively communicate your message across various platforms:

1. **Use a variety of channels:** Utilize traditional media outlets, social media, grassroots efforts, and direct voter engagement to disseminate your message. Each channel offers unique opportunities to reach different segments of your target audience.
2. **Stay on message:** Regardless of the communication platform or issue being discussed, always relate your statements back to your central message. This will help reinforce your candidate's position and differentiate them from opponents.
3. **Address negative attacks:** Be prepared to respond to any negative claims or insinuations made by your opponents. Ensure your responses are well-reasoned, factual, and consistent with your overall message.
4. **Tell a story:** Craft narratives that humanize your candidate and connect with voters on an emotional level. Share personal experiences and anecdotes that illustrate your candidate's values, principles, and commitment to the issues at hand.
5. **Adapt and evolve:** Monitor the campaign's progress and the response to your messaging. Be prepared to adjust your messaging strategy as needed, considering changing circumstances, emerging issues, or shifts in public sentiment.

ANALYZING THE PLAYS: EFFECTIVE MESSAGING FROM OTHER CAMPAIGNS

In recent years, there have been several examples of political campaigns that successfully employed consistent and compelling messaging strategies. Some noteworthy examples include:

1. <u>Barack Obama's 2008 presidential campaign:</u> With the message of "change we can believe in" and the slogan "Yes, we can," Obama's campaign inspired a diverse range of American voters, including the often hard-to-reach youth demographic. The campaign utilized a decentralized structure and innovative digital strategies to bring its message directly to voters on an unprecedented scale.
2. <u>Emmanuel Macron's 2017 French presidential campaign: Macron's</u> En Marche! movement, with its message of unity and progress, defied traditional political divides and emerged victorious. The campaign's emphasis on optimism, inclusivity, and forward-thinking policies resonated with French voters seeking a break from the political status quo.
3. <u>Jacinda Ardern's 2020 New Zealand general election campaign:</u> Ardern's empathetic leadership and clear communication during the COVID-19 pandemic

bolstered her party's position. Her message of "Let's Keep Moving" conveyed a sense of continuity and progress, appealing to voters who appreciated her government's effective crisis management.

By studying these successful campaigns and applying their strategies to your own, you can craft a messaging strategy that resonates with your target audience and propels you or your candidate to victory.

PLAYING DIRTY: ATTACK ADS AND NEGATIVE CAMPAIGNING

As I embarked on my political journey, I quickly realized that there are two distinct paths through which negative issues can emerge within a campaign. The first path revolves around the candidate's personal history, which may have certain unfavorable aspects that demand attention. Such negatives can manifest in various forms, such as youthful indiscretions, financial setbacks like bankruptcy, a DUI incident, tax delinquency spanning several years, tumultuous relationships, or even a campaign blunder. While there are other potential negatives, these examples should give you a clear idea. In most cases, these wounds are self-inflicted, but they often necessitate an explanation to the voters. These situations are commonly referred to as a candidate's "baggage" by consultants.

When faced with negative circumstances, it is always preferable to address them openly and swiftly, ensuring they are left behind as soon as possible. Failing to do so may lead voters to believe that you are attempting to conceal something. If your opponent possesses even a modicum of campaign acumen, you can bet that they have engaged in "opposition research" to unearth any potential dirt on you. It is far better to take preemptive action rather than allowing your opponent to expose these negatives to the voters. You want to be in a position where you can confidently state, "Everyone already knows that—it's old news."

The second source of negative campaign issues arises from external forces beyond your own campaign. These may originate directly from your opponent, the media, your opponent's supporters, or individuals who simply harbor animosity towards you—such as internet bloggers.

Negative campaigning has become increasingly prevalent across all levels of elections because, quite frankly, it works. If it did not yield results, we would not witness its pervasive use. Negative campaign charges typically fall into three distinct categories of attack. The first category consists of personal attacks on the candidate, which usually bear no relevance to the campaign itself. These attacks may focus on age, physical appearance, personal relationships, or any other personal aspect. Ethically, these attacks should never find a place in any campaign.

The second category involves attacks on a candidate's record or policies. In my opinion, these attacks are fair game. While some campaigns choose not to assail their opponent's policies or record and instead focus solely on presenting positive solutions, they fear that negativity will repel voters. However, election results demonstrate the contrary, provided that the facts supporting the attacks can be substantiated. It is valuable to draw clear distinctions between your own candidacy and that of your opponent. Candidates should not dismiss the potential use of these negative issues.

When confronted by an opponent who adopts a negative approach, it is a mistake to remain silent and not respond. Some candidates erroneously believe that by ignoring the charges, they will eventually dissipate. However, if the charges are not viewed as ridiculous by the voters, they are likely to persist. That is precisely why responding is of paramount importance.

There exist several effective methods to counter-attack a negative campaign. Let me share a few examples:

1. Question the motivation of the other side: "They are resorting to these tactics because they know they are losing. It reeks of desperation."
2. Get ahead of the negativity and alert voters: "Beware of the other side's desperate attempts to deceive voters through a negative campaign. Stay vigilant, and the truth will prevail."
3. Transform adversity into opportunity: If accused of being a RINO (Republican In Name Only), redirect the debate to a discussion of who has truly championed Republican values. Most politicians have done little for our party. Accuse them of leading the party astray by excluding those who dare to dissent.
4. Accuse your opponent of failing to communicate with voters:
5. "My opponent has nothing substantial to offer except lies and distortions about this election. In contrast, I have personally engaged with voters through over 1,000 door-to-door visits." (Or any other action that demonstrates direct voter contact.)
6. Expose your opponent's reliance on big money from special interests: "While my campaign has been supported by smaller contributors who seek no special favors, my opponent is funded by powerful special interests, enabling a campaign built on lies and distortions."
7. Uncover logical fallacies in your opponent's assertions: Often, negative charges are taken out of context or based on half-truths. By presenting evidence that supports your position, you can easily refute illogical accusations.

Voters generally disdain candidates who engage in false charges.

Above all, it is imperative to respond to negative charges from your opponent. Assuming they will disappear by taking no action is a grave mistake. Often, opponents will employ surrogates to deliver negative charges, attempting to maintain an appearance of moral high ground. In such cases, it is crucial to hold your opponent accountable for using proxies to propagate their messages. Avoid responding directly to the opponent's surrogate and instead place the responsibility where it truly lies—on your opponent.

When responding to negative charges, employ political rhetoric rather than Shakespearian eloquence. In any political setting, it is best to be less detailed and use emotionally charged language. Allow me to illustrate:

- You have a plan—your opponent has a scheme.
- You have genuine supporters—your opponent has mere stooges.
- You enjoy grassroots support—your opponent is a puppet of special interests.
- You make diligent decisions—your opponent manipulates behind closed doors to deceive voters.
- You strive for the best possible solutions—your opponent has compromised their integrity, selling out to vested interests.
- These linguistic techniques add a persuasive flair to your message. Remember, using concise and impactful words can make all the difference in capturing voters' attention and earning their trust.

Negative media coverage can pose a significant challenge for any candidate. However, there is only one surefire way to overcome it—you must proactively confront it. Consider the unfortunate case of Republican presidential candidate Herman Cain. Running a self-managed campaign with minimal professional staff, he likely did not anticipate the rapid success he achieved. Had he established a competent campaign organization, he could have handled the sexual harassment allegations differently, or perhaps even decided not to run at all.

The story unfolded over several weeks, exacerbated by inconsistencies in his statements. A skilled campaign professional would have thoroughly vetted the candidate from the outset—a crucial aspect of opposition research that extends to scrutinizing one's own candidate. Cain's struggle stemmed from his failure to address the issue head-on when it first emerged.

In the media game, swift and assertive responses are paramount. The laws of human behavior dictate that if a credible source, such as a media outlet, presents a story, most people will assume its credibility unless the accused provides a denial or counterargument. Even if the media outlet includes a statement from you, prepared by your campaign, readers and viewers often overlook it. Instead, they focus on your opponent's charges, accompanied by supporting evidence. Moreover, if they learn that "Mr. Johnny Jones refused to answer any of our questions," they are likely to assume your guilt. It is an inherent human tendency to perceive evasive behavior as a sign of guilt.

Now, let's assume you have chosen to engage with the media. It becomes crucial for the story to allocate sufficient time to present your defense. Readers and viewers should understand: A) the story lacks truth, B) your opponent is distorting facts, or C) you are actively working to resolve the issue. Projecting an image of sympathy or empathy may help sway opinion in your favor.

If the negative attacks originate from bloggers on a news outlet, it is wise to establish a "truth squad" that monitors and promptly responds to these attacks. While not all readers engage in blogging, these platforms do influence the opinions of some voters. It is always prudent to correct any misinformation and ensure accuracy.

Another effective approach is to craft and submit your own opinion letter to a newspaper. The "letter to the editor" column is widely read and provides an excellent avenue for delivering your message. While newspapers have guidelines governing what they can publish, it remains a worthwhile endeavor to respond to negative news articles. However, it is important to heed the sage advice that one should "never fight with anyone who buys ink by the barrel."

Negative media coverage can be challenging, but by seizing control of the narrative and responding swiftly and effectively, you can mitigate its impact. Getting ahead of the story, utilizing the media to present your defense, and countering false information are essential tactics for overcoming negative coverage.

Ultimately, as a candidate, the decision regarding the usage and extent of negative campaign issues lies with you. It is crucial to strike a balance between addressing personal "baggage" proactively and responding to external negative attacks. By adopting a strategic and assertive approach, you can navigate the treacherous waters of negative campaigning and emerge stronger, gaining the trust and support of the electorate.

Remember, in the realm of politics, perception often becomes reality. Therefore, it is vital to shape the narrative, control your messaging, and maintain a consistent and transparent image. The power to influence public opinion lies within your hands, and by utilizing effective communication strategies, you can ensure that the truth prevails over misinformation and negativity.

GAME TIME: BRINGING IT ALL TOGETHER

Example: Let's assume **your district has a population of 70,000**, with **20,000 ineligible voters**, leaving **50,000 eligible voters**. If the *last election had a 75% turnout*, you might *expect a similar turnout, resulting in 37,500 votes cast*. <u>To win, you'll need 18,751 votes (50% + 1).</u> Assuming *two voters per household*, this equates to **approximately 9,380 households.**

However, not every voter you speak to will support your campaign. **If you can persuade *seven out of ten voters*, you'll need to communicate with 27,000 voters or 13,500 households <u>to secure 18,900 votes (27,000 x 0.7) or 9,450 households (13,500 x 0.7)</u>**.

By narrowing down the target audience, you can focus your resources on persuading a smaller yet more critical group of voters. As the hypothetical scenario suggests, a well-thought-out campaign strategy requires an in-depth understanding of your district's demographics, voting history, and expected turnout. This kind of data-driven approach can help you not only map out your campaign but also make it more efficient and targeted.

After identifying the number of votes you need to win, the next crucial step is to identify who those voters are. This entails understanding their demographics, their issues of concern, and how best to reach them. For instance, if your district has a significant number of seniors, healthcare and social security may be top priority issues. Alternatively, if there's a large student population, education and job opportunities might be more pressing.

Understanding the needs and preferences of your voters also informs the best way to engage with them. For instance, seniors might respond better to direct mail and phone calls, while younger voters might be more accessible via social media and email.

As stated, you won't win over every voter you contact. A conversion rate of 70% is an ambitious yet achievable target. But how do you ensure you're contacting the right voters, those who are most likely to be persuaded?

This is where voter profiling and segmentation come into play. Use available data to divide your voters into segments based on their likelihood to support your candidate, their likelihood to vote, and their level of influence in the community. Prioritize those who are most likely to vote for you and those who, while undecided, show a propensity to support your candidate's policies or party. Use the next chapter to build a targeting game that's unrivaled!

Next, ensure you have a robust ground game. This means mobilizing volunteers to canvass neighborhoods, make phone calls, and get out the vote on election day. Your campaign's ground game should be focused on your target voters, ensuring they are informed, persuaded, and ultimately mobilized to vote.

The example above illustrates the importance of a data-driven strategy, but it's essential to remember that data alone isn't enough. Connecting with voters on a personal level, addressing their concerns, and inspiring them with your candidate's vision are crucial elements of a successful campaign.

The importance of a well-organized, well-executed campaign cannot be overstated. From accurately identifying your target voters to effectively mobilizing your ground game, every element of your campaign should be geared towards securing the required number of votes. Remember, at the end of the day, it's about not only reaching voters but also persuading and inspiring them to cast their vote for your candidate.

Your campaign is a marathon, not a sprint. By bringing all these elements together and maintaining a strategic, focused approach, you can cross the finish line with the majority of votes on your side.

FOCUSING ON THE RIGHT VOTERS

Defining Voter Targeting

Winning an election requires not only understanding how many votes you need but also identifying the specific voters you need to persuade to support your candidate. This process is known as "voter targeting." The primary aim of targeting is to recognize the segments of the voting population that are most likely to be receptive to your candidate, enabling you to concentrate your campaign resources on these groups.

Recall from the chapter called "Research" that you were asked to categorize voters into smaller groups, which would come into play during the targeting process. That time has arrived.

The Importance of Targeting Voters

Voter targeting is crucial for two reasons: it helps conserve your campaign's valuable resources (time, money, and manpower) and assists in developing a message that effectively persuades undecided voters.

Conserving Campaign Resources

By creating targeted literature and focusing on specific voters, you can save time and money that would otherwise be spent on individuals who are unlikely to vote for your candidate. By identifying a smaller yet substantial group of voters who are most likely to be swayed by your campaign message, you can allocate your resources more efficiently and reinforce your message until they feel compelled to vote for your candidate.

For instance, if you determine that you need to connect with 33%

of the voters to win, and you can accurately pinpoint those voters, you can achieve your goal with one-third of the resources required for an untargeted campaign. In other words, instead of reaching every voter in the district once, you could focus your efforts on reaching your most probable supporters three times.

Candidates who fail to target their voters effectively have no right to complain about scarce campaign resources.

Persuading Target Voters

The next section will delve into crafting your campaign message. However, before doing so, it's essential to determine the best audience for that message. Identifying your target audience helps you tailor a message that will likely resonate with them.

Remember that as a party or candidate tries to appeal to an increasingly broad audience, their message becomes diluted and less effective. A campaign that promises everything to everyone will ultimately fail to captivate voters.

The goal of targeting is to direct your campaign efforts towards a range of voters that can deliver the number of votes you set as your goal in Chapter 2. If your target audience is too narrow, you won't attract enough votes to win. If it's too broad, your message will become diluted, allowing competitors with a sharper focus to capture parts of your target electorate.

In general, there are three types of voters: your supporters, your opponents' supporters, and undecided voters. Your supporters have already decided to vote for you, your opponents' supporters have already decided to vote for your opponents, and undecided voters, also known as "persuadable voters," need to be convinced to vote for either candidate. Your goal is to target a portion of these persuadable voters and communicate your message effectively.

How to Target Voters

Once you've established that you need to persuade roughly half the electorate or less to vote for your candidate, you must identify what sets your potential voters apart from the rest. This can be done through geographic and demographic targeting, with most campaigns employing a combination of both.

Geographic Targeting

Geographic targeting involves determining who will vote for your candidate based on where they live. It's essential to examine past elections to ascertain previous performance, voter persuadably, and expected turnout. Analyzing data at the precinct level (the smallest geographic area where votes are cast and tabulated) can provide valuable insights.

Past performance indicates the percentage of votes that your candidate, party, or similar candidate received in previous elections. Precincts with high performance contain your most likely supporters.

The persuadably of voters is measured by the percentage of voters in a precinct who do not consistently vote for the same party or candidate. It is the difference in the percentage of votes for similar candidates in the same election or across consecutive elections. Voters either "split" their vote (voting for candidates with different affiliations in the same election) or "shift" their vote (voting for candidates with different affiliations over two or more elections).

"Ticket splitters" and "vote splitters" are generally considered the voters most likely to be persuaded by a campaign's efforts. As a result, most campaigns allocate the majority of their resources—such as posters, door-to-door visits, and more—to constituencies with high persuadably.

Expected turnout can be determined by the percentage of voters who participated in the most recent similar election. It's unwise to spend campaign resources on people who won't vote; thus, your campaign should allocate more resources to precincts with a history of higher turnout.

Demographic Targeting

In addition to geographic targeting, demographic targeting is essential in identifying potential voters. Demographic targeting considers factors such as age, gender, race, income level, education, and other socio-economic indicators to determine which groups of voters are most likely to support your candidate.

By combining both geographic and demographic targeting, your campaign can create a more comprehensive and accurate profile of the voters you need to persuade. This information allows you to tailor your campaign message and allocate resources effectively, increasing your chances of winning the election.

In conclusion, voter targeting is a crucial element in a successful political campaign. By understanding which voters to focus on and allocating resources accordingly, your campaign can optimize its efforts and craft a compelling message to persuade the right audience. By targeting the appropriate voters, you increase your chances of achieving your campaign goals and ultimately winning the election.

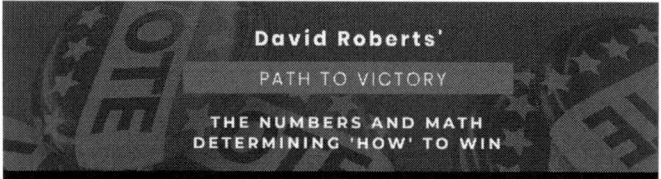

David Roberts' PATH TO VICTORY
THE NUMBERS AND MATH DETERMINING 'HOW' TO WIN

The chart below represents the math and calculations for running for a statewide office in the state of Oklahoma (calculated May 10, 2023) The best campaigns are always the ones with clear strategies and plans. Knowing the numbers is one of the most important early steps in the campaign process.

OKLAHOMA DEMOCRAT PATH TO VICTORY FOR STATEWIDE RACE 2023

Voting Eligible Population	2,875,059	
Registered Voters	1,868,090	
Expected Vote	1,169,274	**Expected Vote**
Vote Goal	608,022	Average of past 2 elections
Baseline	184,020	
Persuasion Universe	221,420	**Win Number**
GOTV Universe	52,044	Expected Vote divided by 2 + 1
VOTE DEFICIT	**424,002**	
		Vote Goal = Expected Vote X .52

Margin of Victory Path

Vote Deficit = Vote Goal - Baseline

Universes	Universe Size	% Needed	MOV Added
Persuasion	221,420	65.0%	143,923
GOTV	52,044	65.0%	33,829
Unregistered	1,006,969	7.0%	70,488
	MARGIN OF VICTORY		**248,239**

Voting Eligible Population: This number (2,875,059) represents the total number of people in Oklahoma who are legally eligible to vote. This includes citizens who are over 18 and not barred from voting for any reason

Registered Voters: This number (1,868,090) refers to individuals who are not only eligible to vote, but who have also formally registered to do so.

Expected Vote: This number (1,169,274) is the campaign's estimate of how many people will actually turn out to vote, based on past elections, polling, and other relevant data.

Vote Goal: This number (608,022) is the total number of votes that the campaign estimates it needs to win the election. This number is usually less than half of the Expected Vote, especially in races with more than two candidates.

Baseline: This figure (184,020) is the number of votes that the campaign is fairly certain it will receive, based on previous voting patterns, polls, and other data. These are likely committed Democratic voters.

Persuasion Universe: This group (221,420) represents the voters who are currently undecided or are weak supporters of other candidates. The campaign believes they can be persuaded to vote for the Democratic candidate.

GOTV Universe: GOTV stands for Get Out The Vote. This group (52,044) consists of voters who are likely to support the Democratic candidate, but who might not vote without encouragement or assistance from the campaign.

Vote Deficit: This number (424,002) is the difference between the campaign's Vote Goal and its Baseline. It represents the number of additional votes that the campaign needs to secure to reach its Vote Goal.

SCOUTING REPORT: YOUR CAMPAIGN'S TARGET AUDIENCE

To construct a robust campaign, it's essential to delve into the heart of your target audience. Examining their values, attitudes, issue priorities, and desired leadership qualities will lay the foundation for a successful campaign strategy.

Values: Uncovering Common Ground

Identify the fundamental values that resonate with your target audience. Assess which they prioritize: social protection or economic opportunity, societal order or personal freedom, stability or reform, peace or police security. Recognize the shared values amongst your target voters and the distinct values that differentiate them from the general population.

Attitudes: Gauging Sentiments

Examine voter outlooks towards the future: are they optimistic or pessimistic? Do they trust or mistrust the government and other social institutions? Assess their current situation compared to the past and determine whether they desire change or stability.

Issue Priorities: Identifying Key Concerns

Determine the issues that will captivate your target voters' attention during the election. Ascertain whether they are primarily concerned with economic, social, or foreign policy issues. Further, investigate the importance of issues such as crime control, business investment, and other specific concerns that may influence voter decisions.

Leadership Qualities: Defining the Ideal Candidate

Unveil the qualities your target audience seeks in a leader. Do they yearn for a stable, experienced figure, or someone young and dynamic who will disrupt the status quo? Investigate whether they prefer leaders with an intellectual background or those who can empathize with everyday people's concerns.

Sociological Research: The Key to Accuracy

Whenever possible, underpin your voter analysis and targeting with rigorous sociological research. Campaigns lacking solid research risk missing crucial insights. Politicians often assume they instinctively understand "the people" but may be surprised by poll results or election outcomes.

Utilize focus groups and political polling to refine your campaign strategies. Focus groups provide qualitative insights into voter values, attitudes, and concerns, while political polling offers quantitative data. Although this document does not delve into the intricacies of sociological research, some polling materials are available in Appendix D.

WORKSHEETS: CREATING A COMPREHENSIVE TARGETING STRATEGY

Developing a thorough targeting strategy entails answering critical questions concerning geographic and demographic targeting. Merge your findings to create a comprehensive voter profile, encompassing their values, attitudes, issue priorities, and desired leadership qualities. Prioritize the factors most likely to influence your target voters in the upcoming election and incorporate these insights into your written campaign plan. This in-depth understanding will serve as a sturdy foundation for a successful political campaign.

Campaign Targeting: A Holistic Approach

A comprehensive targeting strategy is crucial for shaping a political campaign that resonates with the right voters. By addressing questions related to geographic and demographic targeting, you can create a cohesive voter profile that encompasses their values, attitudes, issue priorities, and desired leadership qualities. Use these insights to craft a campaign plan that appeals to both likely and potential supporters.

Geographic Targeting: Zone In on Key Areas

To determine the geographic targeting for your campaign, answer the following questions:
1. Where do all the candidates reside? Are there any distinct geographic areas of support for any particular candidate?
2. What were the outcomes for similar candidates in each precinct of the district in past elections?
3. What is the level of persuadably of voters in each precinct of the district?
4. What is the anticipated voter turnout for each precinct of the district?

Demographic Targeting: Pinpoint Your Core Demographics

To establish your campaign's demographic targeting, consider these questions:
1. What are the demographic profiles (age, gender, profession, education, etc.) of all viable candidates, including your own?
2. Which demographic groups should support your candidate?
3. Are there sufficient votes within these groups to win the election?
4. Where do these demographic groups gather? How do they access information?
5. Are there other candidates appealing to the same demographic groups?
6. Which demographic groups will you concede to your opponents?
7. What collateral groups might you appeal to if necessary?

INTEGRATING ALL TARGETING ELEMENTS: YOUR GAMEPLAN BLUEPRINT

Answer the following questions and integrate your findings into your written campaign plan:
1. List all likely supporters, both geographically and demographically.
2. List all potential supporters, both geographically and demographically.
3. List all unlikely supporters that you will concede to your opponents.
4. What values do both likely and potential supporters hold? Are there any significant differences?
5. What are their attitudes?
6. Which issues concern these voters?
7. What leadership qualities are they looking for?
8. Which responses to questions 4 through 7 are most likely to be the critical factors influencing your target voters in this election?

By following this holistic approach to voter targeting, you'll create a political campaign that effectively speaks to the hearts and minds of your target audience. This comprehensive understanding will lay the groundwork for a successful and engaging political campaign.

CREATING AND LEADING A WINNING TEAM

In the political arena, whether as a candidate or campaign manager, it's crucial to know how to build and lead a team. So, what type of leader should you be, and what are you looking for in others? We often assume the leader is the person everyone turns to, which sometimes looks like a bottlenecked process. What does it feel like to be the blocked message in the middle? What happens if the communication gets stuck?

On the flip side, we might assume that leadership means everyone operates independently, which can lead to a lack of coordination. This approach rarely works. So, who's responsible for coordinating everyone? Who pushes the group forward when a decision can't be reached? Who takes ultimate responsibility for the outcome?

In Democratic campaigns, every Organizer is a leader and held accountable for their designated area. We expect you to coordinate and empower volunteers to take leadership, which requires delegating responsibility (rather than just tasks) and holding others accountable for carrying out that responsibility.

Our model of leadership is represented by the shape of a snowflake, where the leader is in the center, but is not the only focal point. The snowflake model also signifies delegation, shared responsibility, and teamwork.

Volunteers have the relationships and local knowledge you can't learn in just a few weeks. In some areas of your state, the Democratic Party has established team leaders that have been organizing fully-functioning teams for several years. In other areas, there are leaders without an active team. And in some cases, there are volunteers with leadership potential, but no team structure.

A competent Organizer's job is to reach out to the leaders or potential leaders in the community who can recruit and coordinate others well. These leaders will be the backbone of your operation. You must be able to trust them to delegate responsibility to other dedicated, reliable people and to follow through on commitments. You may be the leader in the middle, guiding volunteer efforts and being held accountable for outcomes, but you will be deeply reliant on your relationships with others for success.

WHY CREATE TEAMS?

Our organizing principles rest on the staunch belief that individuals possess the power to transform their communities, and by banding together, they can enact change across their nation. This approach respects, empowers, and includes every community member in our work, using a strategy that is people-focused and driven by key metrics.

Creating and sustaining a volunteer leadership structure is vital to successful organizing. The team model acknowledges volunteers' desire for camaraderie, shared purpose, and intensive training to foster a successful program. During past successful campaigns, organizers capitalized on the enthusiasm and skills of countless supporters, transforming that energy into action led by the volunteers themselves. At the heart of this conversion from excitement to action were the volunteer neighborhood teams that executed the necessary organizing to achieve victory. The reasons for team creation are straightforward:

You can't do this alone:

- Successful campaigns cannot make significant impacts without a robust volunteer leadership structure.
- Teams help avoid burnout, feelings of isolation, and becoming overwhelmed.
- No one individual can organize effectively alone.
- It makes sense:
- Teams enable volunteers to take ownership of their work.
- Being part of a team provides a sense of purpose and the feeling of being part of something greater than oneself.
- Sharing responsibilities and resources within a team increases efficiency, enables mutual accountability, and ultimately allows the team to accomplish more.
- Teams allow for outreach spread over a larger geographic area.
- Organizing within familiar neighborhoods utilizes local knowledge and personal relationships, enabling members to adjust their actions accordingly.
- It works!
- Volunteers working in teams have consistently worked more than twice as many hours as volunteers who did not work in teams.
- Teams are more effective in reaching out to the community: making more calls, holding more one-on-one meetings, registering more voters.
- The team model has consistently allowed for exponential growth in the number of voters we can contact.

DAVID D. ROBERTS

EXERCISE:

POLITICAL CAMPAIGN PLAYBOOK

1. What are the names of the volunteer leaders present at our training?

2. Who is the Obama for America State Director/Field Director in our State?

3. What are the names of the staff present at the training?

4. What percentage of voters in our state are registered Democrats?

5. What percentage of voters in our state are registered Republicans?

6. What percentage of voters in our state are registered Independent?

7. What is our state's biggest employer or industry?

8. Who is our Governor? Are they a Republican or Democrat? (Bonus points if you have one fun fact about them)

9. Who are our 2 U.S. Senators? Are they Republican or Democrat? (Bonus points if you have one fun fact about them.)

10. In the 2008 Presidential election, our state voted for _____ for President by _____ points.

11. Our state capitol is:

12. There are _____ counties in our state

13. The states that border ours are:

14. The last time President or candidate Obama visited our state was:

15. The best thing about Obama for America in our state is:

16. The Democratic party chair in our state is named:

CRAFTING A STRATEGIC VOTER ENGAGEMENT PLAN – YOUR FANBASE

Step Five: Designing an Effective Voter Contact Strategy

Having identified your target audience and refined your campaign message, it's time to determine the best approach to communicate your message to the voters. This entails considering the costs, the flexibility of resources and methods, and the overall effectiveness of each approach to persuade, identify supporters, and mobilize voters. A well-planned strategy accounts for every phase of the campaign, from persuasion to the final push on Election Day.

1. **Balancing Finite Resources**

Political campaigns are essentially communication endeavors that rely on three key resources: time, money, and people. The challenge lies in finding the optimal combination of these resources and utilizing them efficiently to maximize your impact on the voters. Remember that each decision has an opportunity cost, and you need to allocate your resources wisely to ensure maximum impact with minimal expenditure.

2. **Interchangeability of Resources and Methods**

Keep in mind that different resources and methods can often be used to achieve the same goal. It's crucial to first determine your objectives, then explore the various approaches available to accomplish them. If one method isn't feasible, another might be. Proper planning is vital, as a campaign without a written plan is more likely to face resource constraints and mismanagement of time.

3. Evaluating the Effectiveness of Voter Contact

Different types of voter contact can achieve three key objectives: persuade target voters, identify supporters, and mobilize your vote. Your campaign must employ methods that, in combination, fulfill these objectives.

Effective persuasion involves consistent communication of your message to your target group, ensuring that they remember and support your candidate. As the election period progresses, the focus shifts from persuasion to mobilizing your identified supporters to vote on Election Day.

To achieve this, you need a reliable method of identifying supporters early in the campaign, as well as a plan to reach them quickly before the election. This requires careful consideration of the costs, targeted outreach, and persuasion potential of each voter contact activity, such as literature drops, literature handouts, mail campaigns, and door-to-door canvassing.

A good strategic voter engagement plan requires a thorough understanding of your resources, the flexibility of methods, and the overall effectiveness of each approach. By carefully balancing these factors, you can develop a powerful voter contact strategy that persuades, identifies supporters, and mobilizes voters, ultimately securing victory for your candidate.

The coming chapters will focus upon the two traditional and most common forms of voter contact: 1. Phone Banking, and 2. Canvassing. The chapter that follows is titled Data – I wish I could explain how important and often overlooked data and proper data gathering, storage and retention is for campaigns and long-term political and party success. If you learn little, or even nothing else about voter contact and campaign-building, learn this: DATA AND DATA MANAGEMENT IS THE MOST SIGNIFICANT TOOL YOU CAN EVER VALUE IN CAMPAIGNING. IT NEEDS TO BE A PRIORITY FOR YOU.

PHONE BANKING

Phone banking serves as a highly effective method for engaging voters and discussing issues that concern them. Although it might not offer the personal touch of canvassing, it still provides an opportunity for volunteers to directly interact with targeted voters. Phone banking can influence a person's inclination to vote when it is strategically targeted, conducted by trained volunteers, and when the volunteers share a common community with the voters they're communicating with. This flexible activity is adaptable across different environments, experience levels, and locations.

EFFECTIVE PHONE BANKING
Phone banking proves most effective when a group of volunteers collaboratively make calls to a shared list of contacts. Group calling tends to yield a higher call volume than individual efforts. Moreover, it's more enjoyable and fosters a sense of camaraderie, increasing the likelihood of volunteers returning. This collective action also promotes shared goals and relationship building within the volunteer network.

Effective phone banking involves certain intuitive skills:
- Being friendly
- Maintaining politeness
- Conveying positivity through the phone
- Exhibiting a natural and neighborly demeanor
- Listening more than speaking
- Not strictly reading from the script

However, some skills require practice:
1. Handling objections and responding effectively
2. Maintaining a friendly tone despite challenges
3. Ensuring the campaign message resonates with voters
4. Succinctly presenting information without losing the essence of the message
5. Adjusting the approach based on the audience (first-time voters vs. volunteers)

HOLDING A PHONE BANK

PHONEBANK TIPS

- Consider what it will be like in your potential location to have a group of people all talking on the phone at the same time- is it a public area where other people will be, and if so, will the phone bankers be a distraction to them? Will they be a distraction to the phone bankers?

- While landlines are ideal for making calls from the office, most locations will not have them, and in some locations we may not be able to use them under FEC rules. Ask your volunteers to bring their own cell phones to use.

- Make sure that your location has cell service before you book it. You will be surprised how many locations have spotty coverage.

- Some phonebankers are old pros. They may resist the role-play or long explanation of the script. Pair them up with the newest volunteer and empower them to be the trainer. This acknowledges their experience while ensuring that they will read any new material.

- Make sure that your volunteers know that the information that they are recording will be transferred into VAN. This helps them to understand why using the codes and writing neatly are better than long hand notes.

- Staple your call sheets into packets of 50 calls. People are much more likely to make all the calls!

- Tallying calls during the phonebank, or having ways for the volunteers to celebrate commitments as they get them will make the phonebank more fun.

- Have people tweet and share pictures on Facebook during the event.

- At the end, ask each volunteer to share a good and a challenging call. This allows you to coach and debrief the hard conversations while also celebrating the successful calls.

- Plan ahead for data entry. If your phonebank is large enough you can have one or two people doing data entry at the event, if you have them start an hour after the phonebank begins. If your phonebank is smaller and your crowd younger, they may be able to use laptops and Virtual Phonebank.

While many volunteer teams can independently conduct their phone banks with minimal staff support, it's crucial for organizers to be proficient in hosting their own phone banks. The preparation for a phone bank includes location selection, volunteer recruitment, and material preparation. As an organizer, you're also tasked with guiding and supporting callers, particularly those new to this kind of activity who may feel apprehensive about discussing important issues with strangers over the phone.

PHONEBANK CHECKLIST

CTM	STAFF	DESCRIPTION	TIME FRAME
		Identify host or team lead for the phonebank	5-7 Days Out
		Establish date and time for the phonebank	5-7 Days Out
		Confirm a comfortable, quiet, ADA accessible location with cell service and access to parking and/or public transit	5-7 Days Out
		Post event details on BarackObama.com	5-7 Days Out
		Send an email to the local grassroots team with details	3-4 Days Out
		Call local volunteers identified in MyCampaign to invite them	2-5 Days Out
		Share event on social networks	2-5 Days Out
		Make confirmation calls to attendees to remind them to come	Day Before
		Send a reminder email to the local grassroots team	Day Before
		Print scripts, call lists, tally sheets, and any other materials	Day Before
		Sign in volunteers & thank them for coming	8 Mins
		Go over the basics of making calls	5 Mins
		Go over the script and any other materials	5 Mins
		Roleplay!	10 Mins
		Set a call goal so that all participants can work toward it together	2 Mins
		Make calls with the participants	2 Hours
		Coach each other on tough calls	2 Hours
		Celebrate successful calls together	2 Hours
		Take pictures, Tweet, & update Facebook with stories, quotes, fun	5 Mins
		Tally and celebrate progress	5 Mins
		Sign up all participants for the next event	10 Mins
		Thank everyone for coming	5 Mins
		Do a final tally and report totals into Dashboard	Day of Event
		Thank volunteers via social networks	Day of Event
		Enter all data into the VAN	1-2 Days After
		Call people who were scheduled but did not attend	1 Day After
		Call participants to thank them and confirm for their next event	2-3 Days After

CANVASSING

A canvass is a coordinated initiative to visit communities door-to-door, engaging voters directly on matters important to them. This face-to-face interaction helps to generate a list of supporters, disseminate information, address any queries about the party's agenda, and ultimately encourage voters to participate in elections.

Conducting canvassing in local neighborhoods is the most impactful way of discussing pressing issues with community members. Time and again, elections have shown that targeted, efficient, and effective conversations occur predominantly through canvassing. Past successes hinge on the campaign's ability to disseminate its message via personal interactions with voters, fostering a sense of community through neighbor-to-neighbor dialogues.

EFFECTIVE CANVASSING

Canvassing is the most potent voter contact tool available, and mastering the art of facilitating high-quality canvassing will be a crucial skill for organizers. Bear the following points in mind when participating in or planning a canvass:

Quantity and quality matter: There are countless voters nationwide that we'll need to engage multiple times before Election Day to meet our objectives. It's important to have quality conversations but also to use time efficiently. Limit interactions to 3-4 minutes per voter. Be friendly and enthusiastic, answer their questions, and then politely move on.

Personalize the script: The provided script outlines key talking points, but your effectiveness will increase when the message is genuinely from you. Sharing your personal story about why you're canvassing resonates more than any pre-defined points.

Avoid providing an "out": Avoid asking open-ended questions like, "Are you still considering your options?" Instead, frame your questions to elicit firm commitments.

Avoid confrontations: Arguing with voters won't change their minds. If there's disagreement, ask open-ended questions to understand their values, then align your advocacy with these values.

Stick to your list: The individuals on your list are registered voters most likely to be receptive to our message. Deviating from this list may lead to time wasted on non-supportive voters.

Be mindful of data entry: Ensure your recorded data is clear and organized, so it can be accurately input into our voter database later.

Elicit firm commitments: When a voter expresses support, don't end the conversation there. Invite them to volunteer or discuss their voting plan if Election Day is near.

Leave literature behind: Our literature is an essential tool to reinforce our message and provide contact information, even when no one is at home.

Complete your packet: Each packet is designed to be completed in a 2-3 hour shift. Plan your route for efficiency and aim to hit every door on your list.

Smile and enjoy the process: Voters respond more positively to someone who appears to be enjoying their work.

HOLDING A CANVASS

The objective of a canvass is to reach as many individuals and secure as many commitments as possible. Use the checklist below to plan your canvass, including identifying a meeting point, encouraging participation, and gathering information.

CANVASS TIPS

- The goal of a canvass is to talk to as many people and collect as many commitments as possible. Therefore, we want to target densely populated areas with lots of our voters. Our door-to-door canvassing should focus on dense neighborhoods that are easily "walkable". You should think about neighborhoods where the houses are relatively close together and we can hit as many doors as possible.

- A kickoff location, where people will gather before and after the canvass doesn't have to be fancy. It can be a private home, park, school, or any other location that will accommodate your group and allow for a brief training. When you create your event on BarackObama.com, be sure to choose the specific event type.

- There are a LOT of materials to prep with a canvass. Make sure you start early and have a solid distribution plan.

- All volunteer canvassers should have three maps:
  - A map that directs them from the kickoff location to the part of the neighborhood that they will be canvassing (Tip: Google Maps!)
  - A map of the part of the neighborhood that they will be walking that day (Tip: VAN!)
  - A map that directs them from their part of the neighborhood back to the kickoff location

- Canvassers should also have a VAN walk list, literature, and a script.

- It is important to remind canvassers that they CANNOT leave literature in a mailbox, but must leave it on or in the door.

- Check in with canvassers by cell phone or by making rounds while they are walking.

- Prepare for the weather. If it is hot, make sure that you have plenty of water. If it is raining, have ponchos, if it is cold offer people hand warmers and coffee.

- Have canvassers put their walk packets back in order after the canvass. It makes data entry much easier.

POLITICAL CAMPAIGN PLAYBOOK

CANVASS CHECKLIST

CTM	STAFF	DESCRIPTION	TIME FRAME
		Identify host or team lead for the canvass	5-7 Days Out
		Establish date and time for the canvass	5-7 Days Out
		Confirm an easy-to-find meeting location near the walk area that will allow for meet up, training, and supply distribution/collection	5-7 Days Out
		Post event details on BarackObama.com	5-7 Days Out
		Send an email to the local grassroots team with details	3-4 Days Out
		Call local volunteers identified in MyCampaign to invite them	2-5 Days Out
		Share event on social networks	2-5 Days Out
		Make confirmation calls to attendees to remind them to come	Day Before
		Send a reminder email to the local grassroots team	Day Before
		Print scripts, walk lists, maps, tally sheets and bundle literature	Day Before
		Prepare clipboards: 1 script, 2 pens, 50 door list, 50 pieces lit, map of canvass, maps from training location to canvass location & back	Day Before
		Sign in volunteers, thank them for coming & give them your cell #	8 Mins
		Pair people up to canvass together & have them exchange cell #s	2 Mins
		Go over the basics of canvassing (knocking, leaving lit, etc)	5 Mins
		Go over the walk list, map, and script	8 Mins
		Roleplay!	10 Mins
		Set a door goal for each participant to work toward	2 Mins
		Canvass with the newest participant	2 Hours
		Take calls from canvassers with questions	2 Hours
		Check in with canvassers and re-distribute materials or water	2 Hours
		Take pictures, Tweet, & update Facebook with stories, quotes, fun	5 Mins
		Collect materials back at starting location	30 Mins
		Tally and celebrate progress with canvassers as they return	30 Mins
		Sign up all participants for the next event	10 Mins
		Thank everyone for coming	5 Mins
		Do a final tally and report totals into Dashboard	Day of Event
		Thank volunteers via social networks	Day of Event
		Enter all data into the VAN	1-2 Days After
		Call people who were scheduled but did not attend	1 Day After
		Call participants to thank them and confirm for their next event	2-3 Days After

DATA

Data is the backbone of our information system. Accurate, comprehensive, and high-quality data enables us to operate effectively at local, state, and national levels. When a field operation possesses accurate and dynamic data, and is propelled by adaptable and intelligent volunteers and organizers, it can adapt, grow, and mobilize more rapidly and effectively than ever before.

Each of us gathers information daily. Every interaction, be it a phone call with a neighbor or an email exchange, generates valuable data. These golden nuggets of knowledge shouldn't be wasted. Each piece of information must find its way to a central database, such as the Voter Activation Network, also known as VAN or VoteBuilder.

VAN tracks activities, gauges progress towards goals, and maintains a detailed history of calls, door knocks, volunteer shifts, stories, and more. VAN maintains a voter file for each state, providing a wealth of information that enables Democratic campaigns to benefit from an accumulated institutional memory. Accessible via the internet, it can support decentralized field campaigns and grassroots activism.

VAN enables us to store, search, and interact with all the data we collect. It stores contact histories, voting histories, and registration data, in addition to up-to-date contact information. For volunteers, MyCampaign offers modules to schedule and track volunteer shifts, event attendance, and personal stories.

MyCampaign is an invaluable volunteer activity tracker containing a wealth of data similar to MyVoters. While MyVoters includes all registered voters in the state, MyCampaign can house records for anyone. It's designed to store volunteers and other data relevant to individual campaigns. The data in MyCampaign is only accessible by our team, whereas the voter file data is more widely available. Records can be transferred from MyVoters as they transition from voters to volunteers or volunteer prospects. Maintaining clean, effective data in MyCampaign requires some effort due to the ability to add, edit, and delete anyone.

VoteBuilder offers a variety of features to maintain effective data on voters and manage volunteers efficiently. In your daily activities, you'll be utilizing various functions in VoteBuilder, such as:

- Updating voter or volunteer personal attributes, such as name or address
- Adding new voters or volunteers to the database
- Removing duplicate records to clean up the data
- Creating lists of potential volunteers for outreach
- Designing walk lists or call lists of voters for door-to-door canvassing or phone banking
- Designing and printing literature to leave at the doors of voters
- Recording contact attempts and results, to keep track of our engagement efforts
- Scheduling volunteers for various activities.

BUILDING A STRONG FOUNDATION

Now that you have identified your political passions, it's time to start building a strong foundation for your career in public service. This means developing a set of skills and knowledge that will enable you to succeed in any political role you take on. The first step is to focus on your education. While there is no one "right" path to a career in politics, a strong education is often a key component of success. This could mean pursuing a degree in political science, public policy, or a related field. However, don't overlook the value of a well-rounded education that includes courses in history, economics, and other subjects that are relevant to the political landscape.

Running for office in high school and college student organizations is a great way to develop the skills and experience needed for a career in politics. These organizations provide a platform for young people to develop leadership skills, build networks, and engage in public service.

If you're interested in running for office in a student organization, the first step is to identify your goals and develop a platform. What issues are you passionate about, and how do you plan to address them? What skills and experience do you bring to the table, and how can you use them to make a positive impact?

Once you have a platform in place, it's important to build a coalition of supporters. This involves networking with peers, faculty, and community members, and developing relationships with key stakeholders. It's also important to listen to the concerns and needs of your potential constituents, and to demonstrate a genuine interest in their well-being.

Running for office in a student organization requires a significant amount of time, energy, and commitment. It's important to be organized, disciplined, and focused on your goals. This means setting clear objectives, developing a campaign plan, and staying on track with your campaign activities.

If you're successful in your campaign, serving in a student organization can be a valuable experience that prepares you for a wider political career. This experience can help you develop skills in public speaking, campaigning, fundraising, and coalition-building, all of which are essential for success in
politics.

As you continue to develop your political career, it's important to stay engaged with your network of supporters and stakeholders. This means maintaining relationships with peers, mentors, and community leaders, and continuing to build your skills and experience through internships, volunteer work, and other opportunities.

Running for office in high school and college student organizations can be an excellent way to build the skills and experience needed for a career in politics. By developing a platform, building a coalition of supporters, and staying focused on your goals, you can make a positive impact on your community and prepare yourself for a wider political career.

In addition to and beyond your formal education, it's important to gain practical experience. Look for opportunities to intern with political campaigns, advocacy organizations, or government agencies. These internships will give you real-world experience and help you build a network of contacts that will be valuable throughout your career.

Another important skill to develop is effective communication. This means not only being able to articulate your ideas and arguments clearly, but also being a good listener. Learn to ask thoughtful questions and really listen to the answers. This will help you build strong relationships with others and develop a reputation as a thoughtful and effective communicator.

Leadership is also a critical skill for success in politics. Even if you don't plan to run for office yourself, you will need to be able to motivate and inspire others to take action. Look for opportunities to take on leadership roles, whether it's in student organizations, volunteer groups, or other settings.

Finally, it's important to cultivate a strong ethical foundation. Politics can be a rough-and-tumble world, but it's essential to maintain your integrity and uphold high ethical standards. This means being honest and transparent in your dealings with others, treating everyone with respect, and always putting the needs of your constituents ahead of your own.

In the pages that follow, we will delve deeper into each of these skills and areas of knowledge, exploring how they can help you build a strong foundation for a career in politics. By the end of this chapter, you will have a better understanding of what it takes to succeed in this challenging and rewarding field.

NAVIGATING THE POLITICAL LANDSCAPE

Politics can be a complex and often challenging landscape to navigate, but with the right skills and knowledge, you can learn to navigate it successfully. In this chapter, we will explore some of the key aspects of the political landscape and provide tips and strategies for navigating them effectively.

One of the first things to understand about politics is the importance of relationships. Building strong relationships with other politicians, constituents, and stakeholders is essential for success. This means taking the time to get to know people, understanding their perspectives and concerns, and finding common ground.

Another important aspect of the political landscape is the media. In today's digital age, media can have a significant impact on public opinion and political outcomes. It's important to understand how to effectively communicate with the media, including developing key messages, responding to media inquiries, and using social media to reach a wider audience.

Campaigns are another critical component of the political landscape. Whether you're running for office yourself or working on someone else's campaign, understanding the nuts and bolts of campaign strategy is essential. This includes developing a campaign plan, raising money, building a strong volunteer network, and using data and analytics to track progress and make strategic decisions.

In addition to campaigns, it's important to understand the legislative process. Whether you're working in government or advocating for policy change from outside, understanding how laws are made and how to influence the process is critical. This includes knowing how to work with legislators, building coalitions, and effectively communicating your message to decision-makers.

Finally, it's important to be aware of the potential ethical pitfalls that can arise in politics. From conflicts of interest to improper use of campaign funds, there are many ways that politicians can run afoul of ethical standards. Understanding the ethical expectations of the profession and how to navigate potential ethical dilemmas is essential for success in politics.

In the pages that follow, we will explore each of these aspects of the political landscape in more detail, providing practical tips and strategies for navigating them successfully. By the end of this chapter, you will have a better understanding of how to succeed in the often-challenging world of politics.

COMMUNICATION AND THE ART OF PERSUASION

In politics, the ability to communicate effectively is essential. Whether you're delivering a speech, engaging with constituents on social media, or negotiating with other politicians, your ability to persuade and influence others can make all the difference.

Effective communication is a critical component of success in politics. Whether you're running for office, working on a campaign, or serving in government, it's essential to communicate clearly and effectively with a wide range of audiences.

One of the most important aspects of effective communication in politics is crafting a compelling message. Your message should be clear, concise, and memorable, and it should speak directly to the needs and concerns of your target audience. Whether you're running for office or promoting a policy initiative, your message should be focused on the benefits you can offer to your constituents or stakeholders.

In addition to crafting a compelling message, it's also important to communicate through a variety of channels. This means engaging with voters and stakeholders through social media, traditional media, public appearances, and other means of communication. Each channel has its own strengths and weaknesses, and it's important to develop a communication strategy that leverages the strengths of each channel.

Another important aspect of effective communication in politics is building and managing relationships with the media. The media can be a powerful ally in promoting your message and agenda, but it's important to build relationships with journalists and media outlets in a genuine and authentic way. This means being responsive to media inquiries, providing accurate information, and building trust and rapport over time.
Effective communication in politics requires careful listening and empathy. Whether you're engaging with constituents or stakeholders, it's essential to listen to their concerns and priorities, and to communicate in a way that demonstrates that you understand and care about their needs.

Through crafting a compelling message, communicating through a variety of channels, building relationships with the media, and listening to the needs and concerns of your constituents and stakeholders, you can increase your chances of success in politics. Whether you're running for office or serving in government, effective communication can help you achieve your goals and make a positive impact on the world.

One key aspect of effective communication is knowing your audience. This means understanding their needs, concerns, and priorities, and tailoring your message to resonate with them. Whether you're speaking to a group of business leaders, a community organization, or a group of young voters, you need to speak in a way that connects with your audience and speaks to their interests.

Another important aspect of effective communication is developing a strong personal brand. This means presenting yourself in a consistent and authentic way, and developing a reputation as a trustworthy and effective leader. This can include everything from your tone of voice to your dress and grooming, and should be consistent across all of your communication channels.

When it comes to public speaking, there are a few key strategies to keep in mind. First, be prepared.

Practice your speech beforehand, and make sure you're comfortable with the content and delivery. Second, use storytelling to engage your audience and make your message more memorable. Finally, be sure to tailor your message to the specific audience and occasion.

In addition to public speaking, social media has become an increasingly important communication channel in politics. It's essential to use social media effectively to engage with constituents, build your personal brand, and communicate your message. This means developing a strong social media strategy, creating engaging content, and using data and analytics to track your progress and adjust your approach as needed.

Conclusion
Effective communication is essential in politics. By understanding your audience, developing a strong personal brand, and mastering public speaking and social media, you can build the communication skills you need to succeed in politics. Whether you're running for office, working on a campaign, or serving in government, your ability to persuade and influence others can make all the difference.

CAMPAIGN STRATEGY AND EXECUTION

Campaigning is a critical component of politics, whether you're running for office or working on a campaign as a staffer. Developing and executing a winning campaign strategy can be challenging, but with careful planning and execution, it's possible to achieve success.

One of the first steps in developing a campaign strategy is to identify your target audience. This means understanding the demographics and characteristics of the voters you need to win over in order to succeed. Once you've identified your target audience, you can develop a message and campaign platform that speaks to their needs and priorities.

Another important aspect of campaign strategy is fundraising. Campaigns can be expensive, and you'll need to raise money to pay for everything from staff salaries to advertising. Developing a fundraising strategy, building a network of donors and supporters, and tracking your progress along the way are all critical components of a successful campaign.

In addition to fundraising, developing a strong ground game is also essential for success in a campaign. This means building a team of dedicated volunteers who can knock on doors, make phone calls, and engage with voters on a personal level. It's also important to develop a strong social media and digital strategy, as more and more voters are using these channels to engage with political candidates and campaigns.

Finally, executing a successful campaign requires careful planning and execution. This means developing a timeline and budget, identifying key milestones and goals, and tracking your progress along the way. It also means being flexible and adaptable, as unexpected events and challenges can arise at any time during a campaign.

Conclusion

Developing and executing a winning campaign strategy requires careful planning and execution. By identifying your target audience, developing a fundraising strategy, building a strong ground game, and executing your plan with precision and flexibility, you can increase your chances of success in politics. Whether you're running for office or working on a campaign as a staffer, a well-executed campaign can make all the difference in achieving your goals.

COMMUNITY INVOLVEMENT AND GRASSROOTS ORGANIZING

One of the most important aspects of a successful political career is community involvement. Whether you are a high school or college student looking to run for office in student organizations or an experienced political professional, being actively involved in your community is essential.

Why Community Involvement is so Important.
Builds relationships: Being involved in your community allows you to build relationships with a wide variety of people, from constituents and volunteers to local leaders and business owners. These relationships can be incredibly valuable in helping you build support for your campaigns, and in developing a deeper understanding of the issues facing your community.

Develops your skills: Community involvement can help you develop a wide range of skills, from public speaking and networking to fundraising and coalition building. These skills can be invaluable in any political career and can help you become a more effective leader and advocate for your community.

Builds credibility: Being involved in your community shows that you care about the issues that affect your constituents, and that you are committed to making a positive difference in their lives. This can help build credibility and trust with voters, and can make you a more effective candidate or elected official.

Helps you understand community issues: By being actively involved in your community, you can gain a deeper understanding of the issues that are most important to your constituents. This can help you develop policy proposals and campaign platforms that are responsive to their needs and concerns.

Provides opportunities for public service: Community involvement provides many opportunities for public service, from volunteering at local non-profits and community organizations to serving on local boards and commissions. These experiences can help you develop a strong sense of civic responsibility and a commitment to public service.

In conclusion, community involvement is essential for anyone interested in a career in politics. By building relationships, developing your skills, building credibility, understanding community issues, and engaging in public service, you can become a more effective leader and advocate for your community. So get involved, make a difference, and build a brighter future for yourself and your community.

Mobilizing and Empowering Grassroots Support

Grassroots support is the lifeblood of any successful political campaign, especially for first-time candidates. It provides the foundation for a strong and engaged voter base that drives campaign momentum. This chapter aims to guide aspiring politicians and campaign managers on how to mobilize and empower grassroots supporters, turning them into a driving force for your campaign.

Understanding the Importance of Grassroots Support for First-Time Candidates

Grassroots support is fundamental for first-time candidates. It involves leveraging the power of local communities, engaging people at a personal level, and utilizing their passion to generate momentum. Grassroots movements are rooted in local issues, which can resonate strongly with the community and create a compelling narrative for your campaign.

For a first-time candidate, building a strong grassroots network can make a significant difference. It can provide you with enthusiastic volunteers, a dedicated voter base, and a network of advocates who can help spread your message more widely. It also creates a two-way conversation, allowing you to stay in touch with the community's concerns and tailor your platform to their needs.

Advice: Start early and engage often. Meet with local community groups, attend community events, and network with local influencers. Use social media to connect with supporters and communicate your message.

Grassroots Success Stories: Inspiring First-Time Campaigns

The political landscape is filled with inspiring stories of first-time candidates who have leveraged grassroots support to achieve stunning victories. From Alexandria Ocasio-Cortez's remarkable win in New York to Pete Buttigieg's rise from a small-town mayor to a presidential candidate, grassroots support has proven to be a game-changer.

Advice: Study these success stories closely. Understand how these candidates connected with their communities, how they crafted their messages, and how they organized their campaigns. Use these lessons to guide your own campaign strategy.

Identifying and Engaging Potential Supporters

Building a grassroots network begins with identifying potential supporters. This includes individuals who share your values, are passionate about your cause, or are affected by the issues you want to address. Once identified, the next step is engaging them in meaningful ways - through town halls, community events, or social media interactions.

Advice: Use data to identify potential supporters. This could be voter registration data, social media insights, or local demographics. Once you've identified potential supporters, reach out to them directly. Make them feel valued and involved in your campaign.

Creating a Strong Volunteer Program

Volunteers are the backbone of any grassroots campaign. They can knock on doors, make phone calls, organize events, and spread your message within their social circles. To create a strong volunteer program, you need to provide clear roles, offer training, and make volunteers feel appreciated.

Advice: Set up a structured volunteer program. This should include a recruitment plan, training sessions, and a communication strategy to keep volunteers informed and engaged. Recognize the efforts of your volunteers regularly to keep them motivated and connected to the campaign.

Leveraging Local Resources and Partnerships

Building relationships with local organizations, community leaders, and activists can help amplify your message and grow your grassroots support. This section will explore strategies for forging these partnerships and maximizing their potential.

Communicating Your Message and Values

To mobilize and empower grassroots supporters, it is crucial to effectively communicate your message and values. This section will provide tips on crafting compelling messages that resonate with your grassroots base.

Providing Tools and Resources for Supporters
Giving your supporters the tools and resources they need to advocate for your campaign is essential. This section will discuss the importance of providing training, materials, and digital resources to help supporters become effective campaigners.

Encouraging Grassroots Fundraising and Advocacy
Grassroots fundraising and advocacy can have a significant impact on your campaign's success. This section will offer strategies for encouraging and nurturing grassroots fundraising efforts, as well as tips for empowering supporters to become vocal advocates in their communities.

Case Studies: Successful Grassroots Campaigns
This section will showcase inspiring examples of successful grassroots campaigns from various first-time candidates across the globe. It will analyze what made these campaigns effective and how they were able to mobilize and empower their grassroots supporters.

Mobilizing and empowering grassroots support is essential for the success of any political campaign, particularly for first-time candidates. This chapter has provided a roadmap for building a strong grassroots network and turning it into a powerful force for change. As you embark on your political journey, remember that the power of grassroots support lies in the passion and dedication of your supporters, who believe in your vision and are eager to be part of the change you wish to bring about.

Community Organizing
Community organizing has been the catalyst behind monumental societal changes for many years. In the last century, it has

emerged as a distinct field with unique strategies and practices. Renowned organizers like Susan B. Anthony, Cesar Chavez, Martin Luther King, and the founders of the organized labor movement all utilized similar tactics to make lasting impacts. They identified a problem, connected with others affected by it, identified the decision-makers with the power to address their issue, and executed specific actions collectively to influence these decision-makers.

Definitions of Community Organizing

The New Organizing Institute defines Engagement Organizing as a powerful approach to instigate change by rallying people around a captivating vision they believe in. This positive change is brought about by campaigns and organizations that identify and develop leaders embedded in all communities.

Historically, these influential organizers have used many of the tools we use today in our organizing efforts, such as sharing personal stories, one-on-one meetings, and house meetings.

Drawing from the pioneering work of community organizers, political campaigns have been able to successfully integrate practices from political organizing with traditional community organizing methods. This successful integration has been demonstrated through numerous electoral campaigns at various levels.

Mary Jane Roberts, author and organizer, simplifies the concept of organizing by defining it as sophisticated relationship building. This stresses the importance of forming and maintaining strong connections with community members in order to effectively mobilize them.

Jeremy Bird, a renowned organizer, emphasizes that there's no distinction between online and offline organizing - there is only organizing. This highlights the importance of leveraging all available channels - digital and physical - to effectively engage with and mobilize the community.

Strategic Advice:
Identify key issues affecting your community and connect with those impacted by these issues.

Leverage personal stories to build empathy and rally support.

Invest in relationship-building with community members and stakeholders. This could involve regular meetings, attending community events, and using social media to engage with supporters.

Incorporate both online and offline strategies in your organizing efforts. This might involve using social media to connect with supporters, while also conducting face-to-face meetings and organizing community events.

Learn from successful community organizing campaigns and adopt their best practices in your campaign.

Develop and empower local leaders who can champion your cause within their circles.

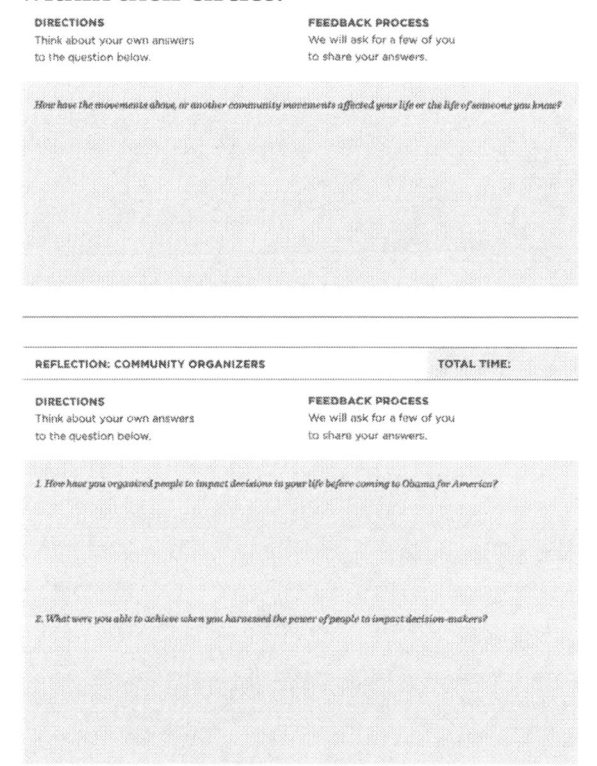

DIRECTIONS
Think about your own answers to the question below.

FEEDBACK PROCESS
We will ask for a few of you to share your answers.

How have the movements above, or another community movements affected your life or the life of someone you know?

REFLECTION: COMMUNITY ORGANIZERS   **TOTAL TIME:**

DIRECTIONS
Think about your own answers to the question below.

FEEDBACK PROCESS
We will ask for a few of you to share your answers.

1. How have you organized people to impact decisions in your life before coming to Obama for America?

2. What were you able to achieve when you harnessed the power of people to impact decision-makers?

EXPECTED CHALLENGES AND ADVERSITY IN POLITICS

Politics can be a challenging and sometimes difficult career path to pursue. In the world of political campaigns, challenges and adversity are inevitable. From navigating the turbulent waters of public opinion to managing unexpected crises, political warfare demands resilience, adaptability, and strategic thinking. This chapter delves into the essential mindset and practical strategies for anticipating, confronting, and ultimately triumphing over the hurdles that arise on the campaign trail. By embracing the inevitable challenges, you can turn them into opportunities for growth and success.

Develop resilience: Resilience is a fundamental trait for any successful political candidate or campaign professional. It involves not only bouncing back from setbacks and failures but also thriving in the face of adversity. To develop resilience, consider the following strategies:

1. Cultivate a strong support network: Surround yourself with a diverse group of individuals who provide emotional support, guidance, and constructive feedback. Seek out mentors, colleagues, friends, and family members who understand the challenges of

politics and can offer perspective during difficult times.
2. Practice self-care: Prioritize your physical and mental well-being. Engage in activities that help you relax, recharge, and maintain a healthy work-life balance. Regular exercise, proper nutrition, quality sleep, and hobbies outside of politics can all contribute to building resilience.
3. Learn from setbacks: View setbacks as learning opportunities rather than failures. Analyze what went wrong, identify areas for improvement, and apply those lessons to future endeavors. Embrace a growth mindset that values continuous learning and adaptation.
4. Develop coping strategies: Identify effective coping mechanisms to manage stress, anxiety, and disappointment. These can include techniques such as meditation, deep breathing exercises, journaling, or seeking professional support when needed.

Be persistent: Persistence is a crucial quality for political candidates and campaign professionals. It is the determination to keep going despite obstacles and setbacks. To maintain persistence:

1. Set realistic goals: Break down your long-term objectives into smaller, achievable milestones. This allows you to track progress and celebrate smaller victories along the way, keeping your motivation high.
2. Stay focused on your vision: Clarify your purpose and keep it at the forefront of your mind. Remind yourself why you entered politics and the positive impact you aspire to make. This sense of purpose can help fuel your persistence and drive.
3. Learn from experiences: Reflect on both successes and failures. Extract valuable lessons from each experience and apply them to refine your strategies and approaches. Embrace a growth mindset that sees every challenge as an opportunity for growth and improvement.
4. Surround yourself with a supportive team: Build a

dedicated and resilient team that shares your vision and values. Collaborate closely with them, leveraging their expertise and support to overcome obstacles collectively.

Build coalitions: Building strong coalitions and alliances is vital in politics. By joining forces with like-minded individuals and organizations, you can amplify your impact and reach broader audiences. Consider the following when building coalitions:

1. Identify common goals and values: Seek out individuals and organizations that align with your political agenda and share similar values. Identify areas of mutual interest and the potential for collaboration.
2. Foster relationships: Invest time and effort in building genuine relationships with potential coalition partners. Attend networking events, engage in discussions, and find opportunities for collaboration. Effective communication and active listening are key to establishing trust and rapport.
3. Find strength in diversity: Embrace diversity within your coalition. Engage with individuals and organizations representing various backgrounds, perspectives, and experiences. This diversity enriches your campaign by offering unique insights, broadening your support base, and ensuring inclusive decision-making processes.
4. Clearly define roles and responsibilities: Establish clear roles, responsibilities, and expectations within the coalition. Create a shared vision and set achievable goals that align with the collective objectives. Regularly communicate and collaborate to maximize the coalition's effectiveness.

Embrace diversity: Recognizing and embracing diversity is crucial for political candidates and campaign professionals. It allows for a more inclusive and representative approach to governance. Consider the following strategies to embrace

diversity:
1. Educate yourself: Continuously educate yourself about the experiences, needs, and perspectives of diverse communities within your constituency. Read, attend workshops, engage in dialogue, and seek opportunities to learn from individuals belonging to different backgrounds.
2. Diversify your team: Build a diverse campaign team that reflects the diversity of the community you aim to represent. Seek individuals from different ethnicities, genders, socioeconomic backgrounds, and age groups. This diversity within your team brings varied insights and helps ensure that your campaign strategies and policies are inclusive and responsive to the needs of all constituents.

3. Engage with diverse communities: Actively reach out and engage with diverse communities within your constituency. Attend community events, forums, and cultural celebrations to listen to their concerns, understand their unique challenges, and build relationships based on trust and respect. Establishing open lines of communication fosters a deeper understanding of their needs and allows you to tailor your campaign messaging and policy proposals accordingly.
4. Incorporate diversity in policy development: When formulating your policy platform, consider the diverse perspectives and experiences of different communities. Take into account the specific challenges they face and propose solutions that promote equity, inclusivity, and social justice. Seek input from community leaders, advocacy groups, and experts who can provide valuable insights and ensure your policies address the needs of all constituents.

5. Foster dialogue and collaboration: Create platforms for meaningful dialogue and collaboration among diverse groups. Facilitate conversations that promote understanding, bridge divides, and build consensus on important issues. Encourage participation from underrepresented communities, ensuring their voices are heard and their perspectives are integrated into decision-making processes.

Focus on the big picture: In the fast-paced and often contentious world of politics, it's crucial to maintain focus on the big picture. This involves keeping your long-term goals and overarching vision in mind as you navigate through challenges. Consider the following strategies to stay focused:

1. Define your mission and values: Clearly articulate your mission statement and core values. These foundational elements serve as your compass, guiding your decisions and actions throughout the campaign. Regularly remind yourself and your team of the broader purpose behind your political engagement.
2. Prioritize key issues: Identify the key issues that align with your vision and have a significant impact on your constituents. Concentrate your efforts on these priority areas, channeling your resources and messaging strategically. By focusing on a few critical issues, you can build expertise, convey a coherent message, and generate tangible results.
3. Seek common ground: While politics can be polarized, look for areas of common ground and shared goals with individuals or groups who may have differing viewpoints. Building bridges and finding commonalities can help foster collaboration and facilitate progress on important issues.
4. Stay adaptable yet consistent: Adapt your strategies and tactics as circumstances evolve, but maintain consistency in your core principles and values. Embrace innovation and new approaches when necessary, but

ensure that they align with your long-term objectives and do not compromise your integrity.
5. Engage in strategic planning: Develop a comprehensive campaign plan that outlines your strategies, objectives, and timelines. Regularly revisit and update this plan as needed, making adjustments based on the evolving political landscape and feedback from constituents. A well-defined roadmap will keep you focused and help measure progress towards your ultimate goals.

Embracing challenges and adversity in political warfare requires developing resilience, persistence, coalition-building skills, embracing diversity, and maintaining focus on the bigger picture. By incorporating these strategies into your campaign approach, you can navigate the complexities of politics with confidence, build meaningful connections with diverse constituents, and work towards achieving your long-term vision of making a positive impact on your community.

THE IMPORTANCE OF ETHICS AND INTEGRITY

In politics, ethics and integrity are essential qualities for success and effective leadership. Unfortunately, politics can also be a field that is prone to unethical behavior, corruption, and a lack of transparency. As a high school or college student interested in politics, or as a seasoned political professional, it's important to understand the importance of ethics and integrity in politics, and how you can uphold these values in your own political career. Here are some key points to consider:

Ethical behavior is essential for building trust: Trust is a critical component of effective leadership and political success. Without trust, it's difficult to build coalitions, inspire followers, or achieve meaningful policy outcomes. Ethical behavior is essential for building trust, as it demonstrates your commitment to honesty, fairness, and transparency in all your actions and interactions.

Ethics and integrity promote accountability: Accountability is another essential component of effective political leadership. By upholding ethical standards and promoting integrity in your actions, you encourage others to do the same. This helps to create a culture of accountability, where individuals are held responsible for their actions, and where transparency and honesty are valued.

Ethics and integrity foster public trust and confidence: Public trust and confidence are critical for political success. When individuals and communities trust their political leaders, they are more likely to engage in the political process, support policies, and participate in civic life. Upholding ethical standards and promoting integrity in your actions can help to build public trust and confidence, which is essential for achieving meaningful political outcomes.

Ethics and integrity are essential for effective decision-making: Effective political leadership requires the ability to make difficult decisions that balance competing interests and priorities. Ethical behavior and integrity are essential for effective decision-making, as they help to ensure that decisions are based on sound principles and values, and that they are made in the best interests of the community.

Ethics and integrity are necessary for long-term success: Finally, ethics and integrity are necessary for long-term political success. While unethical behavior or corruption may provide short-term gains or advantages, they ultimately erode public trust and confidence, and can lead to long-term damage to one's reputation and career.

In conclusion, ethics and integrity are essential qualities for success and effective leadership in politics. By upholding ethical standards, promoting transparency and accountability, and fostering public trust and confidence, you can build a successful and impactful political career that makes a positive difference in your community.

OVERCOMING BARRIERS AND CHALLENGES IN POLITICS

Politics can be a challenging and often frustrating field, with many barriers to success and numerous obstacles to overcome. Whether you're a high school or college student just starting out, or a seasoned political professional, it's important to be prepared for the challenges and obstacles that you may face along the way. Here are some common barriers and challenges in politics, and how you can overcome them:

Lack of resources: One of the most common barriers to success in politics is a lack of resources. This can include a lack of funding, staff, or other resources that are necessary to run an effective campaign or support a policy initiative. To overcome this barrier, it's important to be creative and resourceful in finding alternative ways to achieve your goals. This may involve building coalitions, leveraging social media and other digital tools, or seeking out support from like-minded individuals and organizations.

Opposition and resistance: Another common challenge in politics is opposition and resistance from others who may not share your views or interests. This can include opposition from rival candidates, special interest groups, or other stakeholders who may be opposed to your agenda. To overcome this challenge, it's important to be strategic and proactive in building support for your initiatives, and to engage in effective communication and negotiation with those who may be opposed to your agenda.

Balancing competing priorities: Effective political leadership requires the ability to balance competing priorities and interests, often in the face of limited resources and competing demands. This can be a difficult challenge, but it's essential for success in politics. To overcome this challenge, it's important to be clear and focused on your priorities, and to be willing to make tough decisions when necessary.

Maintaining integrity and ethics: As discussed in Chapter 12, maintaining integrity and ethics is essential for success and effective leadership in politics. However, this can be a difficult challenge, particularly in the face of pressure and temptation to compromise one's values or principles. To overcome this challenge, it's important to be clear and consistent in your values and principles, and to surround yourself with like-minded individuals who share your commitment to ethics and integrity.

Building a strong and sustainable political network: Finally, building a strong and sustainable political network is essential for success in politics. This can involve building relationships with key stakeholders and influencers, as well as cultivating a strong base of support among voters and constituents. To overcome this challenge, it's important to be proactive and intentional in building your network, and to invest in building long-term relationships and partnerships.

In conclusion, politics can be a challenging and often frustrating field, but by being prepared for the barriers and challenges that you may face, and by developing effective strategies for overcoming them, you can achieve success and make a positive impact in your community.

THE IMPORTANCE OF SELF-CARE

Politics can be a demanding and stressful field, with long hours, high stakes, and intense pressure to perform. Whether you're a high school or college student just starting out, or a seasoned political professional, it's important to prioritize self-care in order to stay healthy, balanced, and effective in your work. Here are some tips for practicing self-care in politics:

Prioritize sleep and rest: Getting enough sleep and rest is essential for physical and mental health, as well as for maintaining focus and energy throughout the day. Aim for 7-8 hours of sleep per night, and take breaks throughout the day to rest and recharge.

Stay active and exercise regularly: Exercise is a great way to reduce stress and improve overall health and well-being. Find activities that you enjoy, whether it's running, yoga, or team sports, and make time for them regularly.

Eat a healthy and balanced diet: Proper nutrition is important for maintaining energy and focus throughout the day. Aim to eat a balanced diet with plenty of fruits, vegetables, and whole grains, and avoid excessive amounts of sugar, caffeine, and processed foods.

Set boundaries and take time off: It's important to set boundaries and take time off from work in order to recharge and maintain balance. This may involve setting limits on work hours, taking regular breaks throughout the day, and scheduling time off for vacations or personal activities.

Seek support and professional help when needed: If you're struggling with stress, anxiety, or other mental health issues, don't hesitate to seek support and professional help. This may involve talking to a therapist or counselor, joining a support group, or seeking medical treatment if necessary.

By prioritizing self-care and taking steps to maintain physical and mental health, you can stay healthy, balanced, and effective in your work in politics. Remember that taking care of yourself is not only important for your own well-being, but also for the success and effectiveness of your work.

SCANDAL AND CRISIS MANAGEMENT AND ROLE OF THE MEDIA

As a political leader, politician, and former government official, I understand more than most the significant impact that media coverage does ultimately have on electoral success. The media serves as a powerful amplifier, shaping the reach and perception of my message. However, with this increased visibility comes the exposure to public scrutiny and criticism. It is crucial to navigate the media landscape strategically to protect and enhance my reputation. In this chapter, I will share valuable insights on the importance of media monitoring and its role in managing political reputation and preventing crises.

The Power of Media Monitoring

Working on a political campaign demands constant vigilance, as the public, competitors, and the media alike scrutinize every move. Media monitoring tools offer an invaluable asset in the fast-paced environment of politics, allowing me to anticipate, manage, and respond swiftly to emerging issues. Here are some keyways media monitoring tools can help:

Real-time Crisis Management

In the realm of politics, crises can arise at any moment. Media monitoring tools enable me to stay ahead by tracking news, social media, and online discussions in real-time. By proactively identifying potential crises, I can swiftly respond, minimize reputational damage, and control the narrative surrounding the issue.

Comprehensive Media Coverage

Media monitoring tools provide an extensive view of media coverage, ensuring that I am aware of how my message is being portrayed across different channels. By analyzing media sentiment, key themes, and audience engagement, I can refine my communication strategies and tailor my message to resonate with my target audience effectively.

Competitor Analysis

Understanding the tactics and messaging of my political opponents is essential in staying competitive. Media monitoring tools allow me to monitor their media presence, analyze their communication strategies, and identify potential vulnerabilities or areas for differentiation. This knowledge empowers me to counter their narratives effectively and position myself favorably in the political landscape.

Public Perception and Sentiment Analysis

By monitoring public sentiment and feedback, media monitoring tools provide valuable insights into how my message is resonating with voters. This data helps me gauge the effectiveness of my communication efforts, identify areas of improvement, and address any concerns or misconceptions swiftly. Adapting my approach based on public sentiment allows me to build trust and maintain a positive reputation among constituents.

Influencer Identification and Engagement

Media monitoring tools enable me to identify key influencers, journalists, and opinion leaders who shape public opinion. By engaging with them through personalized outreach, interviews, or exclusive content, I can cultivate positive relationships and increase the likelihood of favorable media coverage. Collaborating with influencers amplifies my message and expands my reach to wider audiences.

Effectively managing political reputation and preventing crises requires a proactive and strategic approach to media engagement. Media monitoring tools serve as an indispensable resource, providing real-time insights, comprehensive coverage, and actionable data to navigate the media landscape successfully. By leveraging these tools, I can anticipate challenges, respond promptly, shape public perception, and ultimately safeguard and enhance my political reputation. Embracing the power of media monitoring will empower me to forge a positive and influential presence in the political arena, bolstering my chances of electoral success.

WHERE I LEAVE YOU & YOUR PATH FORWARD. A LETTER.

As you continued through the final pages of my book, I hope it has provided you with valuable insights, strategies, and inspiration for your political journey. Throughout our exploration of political campaigns, we have delved into the intricacies of messaging, planning, resilience, coalition-building, reputation management, and so much more. Now, as we conclude, I want to leave you with a final message of hope, gratitude, and motivation as you embark on your path forward in politics.

Throughout this book, we have emphasized the immense potential for impact that lies within political campaigns. We have explored the challenges, the setbacks, and the victories that define this dynamic and often unpredictable landscape. From crafting a compelling message to managing crises, we have examined the tools and strategies necessary to navigate the complex world of politics. I hope these insights have armed you with the knowledge and confidence to make a meaningful difference in your community, your country, and the world.

Before we part ways, I would like to express my heartfelt gratitude to you, the reader. Thank you for investing your time and energy into this book, for sharing my passion for politics, and for seeking to make a positive impact through your own political endeavors. It is individuals like you, with a commitment to public service, who hold the potential to shape a brighter future for all.

As you embark on your own political journey, I want to extend my sincerest wishes for your success. May your campaigns be marked by integrity, authenticity, and a steadfast dedication to serving the public. I hope that your contributions to politics, the political process, or our country are characterized by a genuine desire to leave a positive and lasting impact. Remember that every action, no matter how small, has the potential to create ripples of change and progress.

As I leave you with a final message, let it be one of hope and motivation. Politics can be a challenging and often contentious field, but it is also a space of immense opportunity. Each new campaign presents a chance to shape the discourse, champion important causes, and create a better future for generations to come. Embrace the inevitable obstacles as opportunities for growth and resilience. Believe in your ability to make a difference, and let your passion fuel your determination.

In parting, I leave you with a quote that encapsulates the essence of our journey together:

"Endings are not always bad. Most times, they're just beginnings in disguise." - Kim Harrison

Remember that as one chapter ends, another begins. Embrace the endings as opportunities to start anew, to learn, to adapt, and to leave behind a political landscape that is better off than when you found it. With each campaign, may you leave a lasting and positive impact, contributing to the progress and well-being of the communities and country you serve.

Thank you once again for joining me on this journey. I wish you all the success, fulfillment, and joy that come with your political endeavors. May your path forward be marked by purpose, passion, and the unwavering belief that together, we can shape a brighter future.

With heartfelt appreciation and warmest regards,

DAVID D. ROBERTS

David Roberts

ABOUT THE AUTHOR

David D. Roberts

David Roberts is an American political operative, bureaucrat, entrepreneur, author, historian, and economic development official with a history of service in government, on political campaigns and advocacy organizations. Roberts was born and raised in rural Southeastern Oklahoma but seemed to have an extremely modern skill for political affairs at an early age. At 9 years old, he pulled a wagon to pass out pencils and bumper stickers for his state senator, Gene Stipe, then a strong political force in Oklahoma. By the time Roberts was in high school, he was running for statewide office in career and technical student organizations, first being elected as Vice-President of Future Business Leaders of America, with subsequent elections to State President of Business Professionals of America. In 2003 Roberts became the only Oklahoman to be elected as the National President of Business Professionals of America. Roberts' natural skill for politics led him to study political science and take on roles among many of our highest-profile candidates and campaigns including Obama for America, U.S. Senator Blanche Lincoln, Congressman Brad Carson, Governor Brad Henry, Governor Mike

Beebe, Congressman Mark Critz, with intermittent roles with the DNC, DCCC, union-backed political action committees and unions themselves.

Roberts founded a political consulting and government affairs firm in 2020 earning $1.4 million in grant funding for clients that were rural municipal and county governments. Roberts is widely considered an expert in numerous aspects of services considered crucial towards winning an election including executive coaching and debate preparation, speech writing, leadership, development, finance, strategy, voter persuasion, targeting, field and management. Roberts has been writing and collecting materials and knowledge for this book since his first job as an intern in Washington, DC. He currently works as the Director of Development and External Relations for the Oklahoma Democratic Party. He was committed to developing a book that would be useful for students, first time candidates, and campaign managers - a book that combined his lifetime of knowledge from national presidential campaigns and countless statewide and district-based elections in over 18 different U.S. states.

PRAISE FOR AUTHOR

David Roberts' book, "Political Campaign Playbook," is a triumph in the sphere of political literature and a must-read for anyone with a vested interest in the American political system. With his vast experience spanning over two decades in various aspects of politics and government, Roberts has managed to distill his extensive knowledge into this highly informative and engaging tome. The book is a masterclass in understanding the nuances of running for office and managing a political campaign, blending theory with real-world examples in a way that is both accessible and profound. Roberts' approach to explaining complex political scenarios is remarkably clear and concise, making it an essential guidebook for both novices and seasoned political operatives. From planning and strategizing to dealing with unforeseen challenges, "Political Campaign Playbook" covers all aspects of the campaign process in a practical, hands-on manner. It's the kind of book that not only enlightens the reader but also inspires them to think more deeply about the intricacies of the political landscape.

- DR. RONALD LATREDY

PRAISE FOR AUTHOR

David Roberts' Political Campaign Playbook weaves together practical advice, behind-the-scenes insights, and clear explanations of the strategies and tactics that have shaped successful campaigns in the past. The sports-inspired title of the book is a perfect metaphor for the competitive nature of politics and the need for a clear, well-structured game plan to navigate the complex world of elections.The Political Campaign Playbook features portions that serve as a step-by-step guide to building a winning campaign from the ground up, covering every aspect from fundraising and grassroots organizing to digital strategy and media relations. At the same time, he offers valuable lessons and reflections from his own experiences, which add depth and authenticity to the book. Political Campaign Playbook is not only an invaluable resource for anyone considering a run for office, but also a compelling read that offers a fascinating glimpse into the inner workings of the American political machine.

- CHRIS MATTHEWS

BOOKS BY THIS AUTHOR

Totalitarianism (Key Concepts In Political Theory)

Less than a century old, the concept of totalitarianism is one of the most controversial in political theory, with some proposing to abandon it altogether. In this accessible, wide-ranging introduction, David Roberts addresses the grounds for skepticism and shows that appropriately recast—as an aspiration and direction, rather than a system of domination—totalitarianism is essential for understanding the modern political universe. Surveying the career of the concept from the 1920s to today, Roberts shows how it might better be applied to the three ""classic"" regimes of Fascist Italy, Nazi Germany, and the Stalinist Soviet Union. Extending totalitarianism's reach into the twenty-first century, he then examines how Communist China, Vladimir Putin's Russia, the Islamic Republic of Iran, the self-proclaimed Islamic State (IS), and the threat of the technological "surveillance state" can be conceptualized in the totalitarian tradition. Roberts shows that although the term has come to have overwhelmingly negative connotations, some have enthusiastically pursued a totalitarian direction—and not simply for power, control, or domination.

Made in the USA
Columbia, SC
14 June 2023

7cbd2494-4e44-41dd-ae8d-f573498128e7R01